History of the Pequot War

The Accounts of Mason, Underhill, Vincent and Gardener on the Colonist Wars with Native American Tribes in the 1600s

By Charles Orr

Published by Pantianos Classics

ISBN-13: 978-1-78987-029-9

First published in 1897

Contents

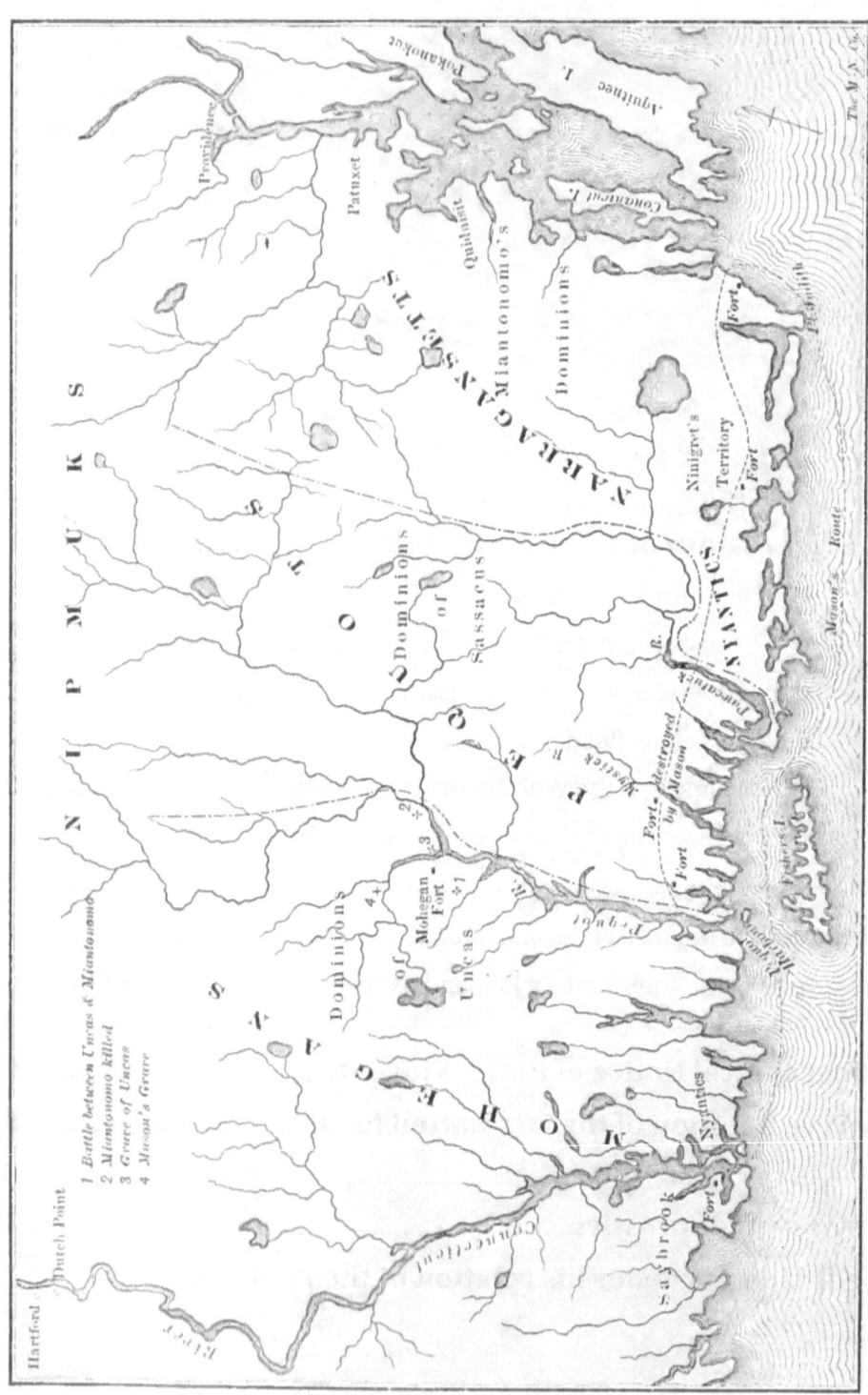

Prefatory Note

The increasing demand for full and accurate reprints of early narratives, contemporary with the events they describe, is an interesting feature of the present revival of interest in American history. The originals of many of these earlier narratives are, of course, now very rare, and to be found only in special collections or in the largest libraries. Much of the more valuable material has been reprinted from time to time by printing clubs and historical societies; but these reprints themselves have, in many cases, become scarce or inaccessible. This may be said of the narratives brought together in this volume, of which only two have before been reprinted in full in separate form. They have, however, all been reprinted in various volumes of The Massachusetts Historical Society *Collections,* and it is from this source that the present publication is made, with the kind permission of the Society. The text, as found in the *Collections,* has been followed closely, and the order of publication preserved; most of the notes have been retained and a few added, mainly in Mason's Narrative, to which prominence is given for apparent reasons. It was thought best to include the biographical sketch of Vincent for the reason that at the time of the original publication of his account of the war nothing was known of its author, nor had anything been discovered up to the time of its publication in the *Collections.* The map is reproduced from George E. Ellis' *Life of John Mason* in Spark's *Library of American Biography.*

C. O.

Introduction

It may be truthfully said that no event in the very early history of New England had a greater influence on its destiny than that known as the Pequot War. It turned the tide which threatened to overwhelm the colonies, and established a peace that continued unbroken for nearly forty years.

So long as the settlements of New England clustered around Massachusetts Bay, and occupied territory from which the Indians had been swept by the terrible plague of 1616-17, the conflict for the possession of the more fertile country to the west was deferred; but when in 1636 the emigrants from Watertown, Dorchester and Newton had pushed their way through the dense forests, and occupied the Connecticut Valley, a struggle for existence became inevitable. For these settlers found the country dominated by the Pequots, the most dreaded of all the tribes of New England, and who had driven away the weaker tribes or held them under subjection.

The earliest known territory of the Pequots was a narrow strip of coast extending from Niantic River to the Rhode Island boundary. They controlled, however, all the tribes east of the Connecticut River, and westward to near New Haven, and nearly all of Long Island. They originally formed one tribe with the Mohegans, who later seceded under Uncas, and remained the faithful allies of the colonists Their total strength at that time is estimated to have been about three thousand; their chief sagamore was the wily Sassacus, and their principal stronghold was at the mouth of the Thames.

The colonists had no doubt given good cause for the hostility of this savage tribe, whose real grievance dated from the seizure, by Thomas Hunt, of twenty-seven inoffensive Indians who had trusted in his honor. For, though this occurred in 1614, [1] it still slumbered in the breasts of Sassacus and the Pequots, who were unable to discriminate between the act of this unprincipled adventurer and the more peaceably disposed settlers of the later period. The incidents leading up to a formal declaration of war by the colonies have been related in detail by Prince in his introduction to Mason's Narrative, by Mason himself and by other contemporaries and later historians. Some thirty persons belonging to the settlements of the Connecticut River and in the Pequot's territory had fallen victims to Indian barbarity; and it was clear that they intended to so harass the settlers as to drive them from the country. There were then in Connecticut some two hundred and fifty Englishmen with their families and they soon became thoroughly aroused as to the importance of aggressive measures. It was the first real emergency the General Court of that colony was compelled to meet. [2] The Court wrote to Massachusetts, February 21st, 1637, for the aid of that colony and making known its intended action. At a special session on the first of May, 1637, offensive war was declared by Connecticut, and by order of the Court a force of ninety men was levied and provisioned; the company was placed under the command of John Mason The solemnity and sadness of the hour may be faintly realized when it is remembered that a failure of the expedition meant perhaps complete annihilation of the settlers and their families. The record of the Court is as follows:

The first day of May, 1637, Genrall Corte ait Harteford.

Mr. Ludlowe, Mr. Wells, Mr. Swaine, Mr. Steele, Mr. Phelps, Mr. Warde.

Committees. — Mr. Whytinge, Mr. Webster, Mr. Willms, Mr Hull, Mr. Chaplin, Mr. Talcott, Mr. Hosford, Mr. Mychell, Mr. Sherman.

It is ordered that there shalbe an offensiue warr ag l the Pequoitt, and that there shalbe 90 men levied out of the 3 Plantacons, Harteford, Weathersfield and Windsor (vizt) out of Harteford 42, Windsor 30, Weathersfield 18 vnder the Comande of Captaine Jo:Mason & in Case of death or sicknes vnder the Comande of Rob'te Seely Leift, & the 'ldest S r ieant or military officer survivinge, if both these miscary.

It is ordered that Harteford shall send 14 Armour in this designe, Windsor 6.

It is ordered that there shalbe l hh of good beare for the Captaine & M r & sick men, if there be only 3 or 4 gallons of strong water, 2 gallons of sacke.

It is ordered that Windsor shall p r uid 60 bushells of Come, Harteford 84 bnshells, Weathersfield 36 bushells, of this each plantacon to bake in biskett the on half if by any meanes they cann, the rest in grounde meale. Weathersfield tenn bnshells to bee allowed vppon Accompt.

Harteford is to pruide 3 firkins of suett, 2 firkins of Butter, w th y* all Rivers mouth, 4 bushells of Oate meale, 2 bushells of Pease, 500 of fish, 2 bushells of salt; Weathersfield 1 bushell of Indian Beanes; Windsor 50 peeces of Porke, 30 lb of Rice, 4 Cheeses.

It is ordered that every souldier shall cary w th him l lb powder, 4 lb of shott, 20 bulletts; 1 barrell of Powder from the Riuers mouth (a light) Gunn if they cann.

(It is ordered) y* Mr. Pincheons shallopp shalbe taken to be imployed (in this desi)gne.

Later records of the Court, referring to the War, show the determination on the part of the settlers to exterminate the Indians and to follow up the advantage gained by the first onslaught.

June 2d, 1637. A General Corte att Harteford.

It is ordered yt there shalbe sent forth 30 men out of the seu r all plantacons in this River of Conectecott to sett downe in the Pequoitt Countrey & River in place convenient to maynteine o r right y 1 God by Conquest hath given to vs, & Leiftenn* Seely shall hauee the Comande of them. The men are to be raised 14 out of Harteford, tenn out of Windsor, 6 out of Wytheresfeild.

It is ordered yt 60 bushells of Corne shalbe p r uided for the designe aboues d , Windsor 20, Harteford, 28, Wythersfeild 12, l hh of Pease, 2 bushells of Oatemeale. 150 pounde of Beefe, 80 lb of Butter (vizt) Windsor 30, Wythersfeild 30, Harteford 20, fish.

26 Jane 1637, Harteford Gen'all Corte.

It is ordered that 10 men more shalbe levied out of the plantacons aforesaide to goe to the designe ag f the Pequoitts as an adition to the form r 30, (vizt) 5 out of Harteford, Windsor 3, Wythersfeild 2.

It is ordered y 1 Mr. Haine & Mr. Ludlowe shall goe to the mouth of the River to treate & Conclude w th o r frendes of the Bay either to joine w th their forces in p r secutinge or designe against o r enemies or if they can see cause by aduise to interprise any Accon accordinge to the force we haue. And to Parle w th the bay aboute o r settinge downe in the Pequoitt Countrey.

It is ordered yt there shale be 1 hogg p r ovided att Wythersfeild for the designe in hande, w ch is concerned to be Nathaniell Footes, 20 lb of butter, half C of Cheese; Harteford 20 lb of Butter, half C. of Cheese, 1 gallon of stronge Water; Harteford 1 C of beefe from Mr. Whittinge, Windsor 3 bushells of mault, 2 deom Wythersfeild, Mr. Wells 2.

The colonies of Massachusetts and Plymouth realized the importance to themselves of aggressive warfare against the encroachment of the savages and responded to the plea of Connecticut. Massachusetts at a special session of her General Court held April 18th, 1637, ordered a levy of one hundred and sixty men and appropriated the sum of six hundred dollars.

This Court being assembled for the speciall occation of psecuting the warr against the Pecoits, it was agreed & ordered, that the warrs, haveing bene vndertaken vpon iust ground, should bee seriously psecuted , & for this end there shalbee 160 men pvided to bee chosen out of the severall townes according to the pportion vnderwritten, vdli; *out of*

Newberry,	8	men o			Charlestowne,	12	more after	4	16
Ipswich,	17	more after	6	23	Boston,	26		9	
Salem,	18		6	24	Roxberry,	10		3	
Saugust,	16		5	21	Dorchester,	13		4	
Watertowne,	14		5	19	Waymothe,	05		2	
Newetowne,	09		3	12	Hingham,	06		2	
Marbleheade,	03		1	4	Meadfoarde,	03		1	

the men to bee named by the several townes, & psented to the counsel, wthin one weeke, who shall give a call vnto such of them as they may thinke fit, (& may impress such as are not freemen, at their discretion,) to the number of 120 at the least; (these who were lately sent to Saybrooke to bee accounted of said number of 160) and they shall pvide amonge these men some fit to bee chosen officers, & such as shalbee enrolled for this service shall have, every common souldier, 20 sh p month, every sergeant, 30 sh p month, besides their dyots, & that the counsel shall take order herein for all other things concerning the said expedition, so as all may be in readiness (so farr as is possible) be the end of the next Generall Court, and for training and ppareing the souldiers, before they bee sent. /

And for the furtherance of this expedition there shalbee 600 levyed fourth w th, according to the last levy of 300. /

The counsell are also to treat w th our neighbours of Plimoth about such ayde as they will send with vs, & also wth or frends vpon Conecktecot, & shall have power to proceede wth them in the said treaty as occation shall require. /

And they shall make choyce of a fit man to bee steweard for makeing & dispencing the pvisions, who shall have 40 sh s the month for wages, beside dyot. /

Capt Trask shall have the comaunde of all the souldiers, & Leift Damport, who shalbee allowed, the capt 6 1 p month, & the leift 4 1 p month; & the next Court will take order for such other comaunder or comaunders as they shall thinke fit to ioyne vnto them. /

The Court of Plymouth Colony passed the following order June 7th, 1637:

Before William Bradford,	Edward Winslowe,
Captaine Miles Standish, gent.,	John Jenney, gentlemen,
Gounor,	Thomas Prence,
Tymothy Hatherley, and	

justice of the peace of o r souaigne lord the kinge, and Assistants in the goument.

It is concluded and enacted by the Court, that the colony of New Plymouth shall send forth ayd to assist them of Massachusetts Bay and Conectacutt in their warrs against the Pequin Indians, in revenge of the innocent blood of the English w ch the s d Pequins haue barbarously shed, and refuse to giue satisf accon for.

It is also enacted by the Court, that there shalbe thirty psons sent for land service, and as many others as shalbe sufficient to manage the barque.

Lieftennant William Holmes is elected to goe leader of the said company.

Mr. Thomas Prence is also elected by lott to be for the counsell of warr, and to goe forth w th them.

The names of the Souldiers that willingly offer themselues to goe upon the sd Service, wth Mr. Prince & the Leiftent.

Voluntaries.

Thomas Clarke,
Richard Church,
Constance Southerne,
John Barnes,
Mr Nathaniel Thomas
& his Mr Goarton,
[man John Cooke, if his famyly can be
puided,
Mr Steephen Hopkins,
John Heyward,
Thomas Williams,
Nicholas Presland,
Thomas Pope,
Phillip Delanoy,
Francis Billington,
Henry Willis,
Perregrine White,
Caleb Hopkins,
Samuell Nash,
Robte Mendall,

Henry Sampson,
Georg Soule,
Samuell Jenney,
Thomas Redding,
Loue Brewster, or
Joseph Robinson, his man
Edward Holman,
William Paddy,
John Hearker,
Richard Clough,
Henry Ewell,
Joseph Biddle,
William Tubbs,
George Kennerick,
Thomas Halloway,
John Irish,
John Jenkins,
Jacob Cooke, Giles Hopkins, John Phil-
lips, Thomas Goarton.

Such as will go if they be prest

Mr Thomas Hill, James Coale, Thomas Boardman,

It is also enacted by the Court, that Mr. Hopkins and John Winslow for the town of Plymouth, Mr. Howland and Jonathan Brewster for the towne of Ducksborrow, and Mr. Gilson and Edward Forster for the towne of Scituate, shalbe added to the Gounor and Assistants to assesse men towards the charges of the souldiers that are to be sent forth for the ayde of the Massachusetts Bay and Connectacutt.

Connecticut raised her levy of ninety men, and Mason started with his expedition on May 10th. The details of the campaign are related in the narratives themselves, and need be only briefly mentioned here. The route taken by Mason may be traced by aid of the map. He sailed down the Connecticut River to Say brook, from whence he was to proceed to the Pequot River and to attack the fort from the west. But he chose to disobey this order, and his reasons are given in his account of the expedition. Having resolved to make the attack from land he sailed at once for Narragansett Bay. The boats reached their destination Saturday evening, the twentieth, and the men remained on their vessels, religiously observing the Sabbath. On Tuesday evening they disembarked, and on Wednesday morning Mason received a message from Roger Williams announcing the arrival at Providence of a Massachusetts party of forty men under Captain Patrick, and requesting him to wait until they came up But Mason decided to push on, wishing to take the enemy by surprise, and with seventy seven white men, (thirteen having been left in charge of the boats), about sixty Mohegans, and two hundred or more Narragansetts, again took up his march. In the evening they came to a fort occupied by the Niantics, a tribe of the Narragansetts. Mason, suspecting them of treachery, caused this fort to be surrounded, in order that they might not convey information to the Pequots. The next morning, some two hundred of them joined the little army, making five hundred Indians in all. At eight o'clock, Mason with his seventy-seven white men and their noisy escort of Indians, was on the march. It was Thursday, the fifth of June in our calendar, and the air was very warm and oppressive. Some of the men fainted on the way on account of the excessive heat and a lack of food. Pawcatuck River was reached after a hard march of twelve miles, and here they rested and refreshed themselves with their mean commons." As they reached the frontier of the Pequots, the Narragansetts began to show signs of fear, and many of them returned to their own country. The company halted again at a point about three miles beyond the Pawcatuck, and held a council. It was found that the Pequots had two forts in this locality, one of which was near the Pequot River and could not be reached before midnight. It was resolved to attack the nearest one, on the Mystic River, and to encamp for the night at Porters Rocks. The camp was a short distance from the fort and they could distinctly hear the shouts of the Indians, who were exulting over the fear of the white men to attack them: for the Indians had seen the expedition pass the mouth of their river a few days before, and did not suppose they would return to attack them by land. At about three o'clock in the morning, the English arose, and after prayers for the success of the undertaking began their silent march for the fort. The Indiana llies were now far in the rear, and Mason had some difficulty in preventing a retreat. He urged them, however, to '' stand at what distance they pleased and see whether the English would fight or not."

The fort, though rude in construction, was quite formidable, considering the great disparity in numbers. It was circular in form, and about two acres in extent and contained about seventy wigwams arranged in rows or streets. It had but two openings: these were on opposite sides and were made difficult of entrance by the use of branches of trees. As they approached the fort, it was agreed that Captain Underbill should enter by one of these openings, while Mason entered by the other. When Mason was within one rod of the opening on the northeast side, the Indians were aroused by the barking of a dog. But Mason, aided by Lieutenant Seeley, pushed aside the brush which obstructed the passage, and entered. the fort with sixteen of his men. Underhill entered from the other side at about the same moment.

The Indians were panic stricken by the suddenness of the attack, and the English used their swords and muskets with deadly effect. By a quick resolve of Mason, fire brands were applied to the inflammable material of the wigwams, and the whole interior was soon a mass of flame and smoke. The English then encircled the fort and the Indian allies formed an outer circle to prevent the escape of any fugitive.

Of the Pequots, between six and seven hundred perished in the fort, seven escaped and seven were captured. Of the English, only two were killed and twenty wounded.

Nothing could be more dreadful than the slaughter and burning on that eventful night; it forms a page in our history too terrible to dwell upon, except in the light of its results, and this was the attitude of all the early settlers toward the event; they believed that there was justification for extreme measures and that the end justified the means.

John Fiske, in his *Beginnings of New England,* says, writing of the overthrow of the Pequots and its importance in the planting of New England: "As a matter of practical policy, the annihilation of the Pequots can be condemned only by those who read history so incorrectly as to suppose that savages, whose business it is to torture and slay, can always be dealt with according to the methods in use between civilized peoples. A mighty nation like the United States is in honor bound to treat the red man with scrupulous justice and refrain from cruelty in punishing his delinquencies. But if the founders of Connecticut, in confronting a danger which threatened their very existence, struck with savage fierceness, we cannot blame them. The world is so made that it is only in that way that the higher races have been able to preserve themselves and carry on their progressive work."

Mason now marched with his little band toward the Pequot River where they were to meet their vessels. They were almost destitute of food and ammunition, and still in the enemies' country. They were attacked by about three hundred of the Pequots from the other fort but were able to keep them at bay, and soon had the pleasure of seeing their vessels sailing into the harbor. They found here Captain Patrick, who had embarked on board the vessels at the Narragansett with forty of the Massachusetts troops. Mason, with twenty of his men, and Patrick with his forty, set out to Saybrook fort by land, while Underhill with the wounded and the remainder of the Connecticut troops went by water. The whole company was royally entertained by Lieutenant Gardener at the fort. Mason then took his men up the river to their homes. There was of course, great rejoicing among the settlers on the Connecticut: for though the danger was not entirely over, it was felt that Mason and his men had dealt a blow which would destroy the power of the Pequots.

Later events were comparatively unimportant and need not be dwelt upon here. It will be noticed that Massachusetts and Plymouth Colonies gave no aid to Connecticut at the critical time of the campaign as conducted by Mason, and of the one hundred and sixty men raised by Massachusetts, only about twenty reached the scene in time to join Mason in the attack. Indeed, Mason does not mention in his narrative the intended union of the three colonies. Their failure, however, to join with Connecticut was due partly to unavoidable delays and partly to the impatience of Mason, which, had it not resulted favorably, would seem little short of foolhardy. But the part he played, and the success of the expedition in which he was the leader, made him without question the hero of the war and placed him on the roll of New England's great men. For the same reason, his account of the war, and particularly of the attack on Mystic fort, is the most interesting of all the narratives. It has distinctly the flavor of actual participate in the events, which is not true of any of the other accounts, except that of Underhill.

Tyler, in his *History of American Literature*, says of Mason's account that it is "a plain but vigorous narrative of a very plain and very vigorous campaign. Naturally enough, the historian writes not from documents, but from his own recollections of the events in which he bore so large a part. His style is that of a fighter rather than a writer; there is an honest blunt ness about it, an unaffected, rough simplicity, a manly, forth-rightness of diction, all the charm of authenticity and strength. It is fortunate that he dashed off this little book without the expectation of printing it. ' I never had thought that this would come to the press...; if I had, I should have endeavored to put a little more varnish upon it.' We like his bluff narrative all the more because the varnish was left off; and we like him all the more as we get acquainted with the modest and frank spirit in which he wrote it. 'I shall only draw the curtain,' he says, ' and open my little casement, that so others of larger hearts and abilities may let in a bigger light; ' that so, at least some small glimmering may be left to posterity, what difficulties our forefathers met with in their first settling these desert parts of America."

[Bibliographical Note. — This narrative was first printed, in part, by Increase Mather in his Relation of the Troubles in New England, 1637, as being the work of John Allyn. It was printed in full from the original manuscript, with an introduction by Thomas Prince, in 1736. A copy of the title-page of this edition will be found opposite. This reprint is made from 2 Mass. Hist. Soc. Coll. vii., 120-153. A reprint was made by Sabin in 1869.]

Notes

[1] In 1614, Captain John Smith, the celebrated navigator, after touching at several places on the coast of New England, embarked for England and left his ship under the command of Thomas Hunt, to load with fish for Spain. Hunt, under the pretense of trading with them, enticed into the ship twenty Indians from Patuxet

and seven from Nanset. He seized on these unsuspecting natives, confined them in the hold of the vessel and carried them to Malaga, where he sold a number of them for twenty pounds a man; and would have disposed of the whole in the same way if the monks of that city had not compassionately interfered and rescued those who remained out of his hands. — i. Mass. Hist. Coll., VII., from Mather's Relation of the Troubles in New England, etc.

[2] The Assembly further showed its consciousness of separate existence by declaring an offensiue warr agt the Pequoitt,' assigning the proportions of its miniature army and supplies to each town and appointing a commander * * * * So complete are the features of State-hood, that we may fairly assign May r, 1637, as the proper birthday of Connecticut." — A Johnston. *The Genesis of a New England State.*

A Brief History of The Pequot War

Especially of the memorable Taking of their Fort at Mistick in Connecticut in 1637.

Written by *Major John Mason,* a principal Actor therein, as then chief Captain and Commander of Connecticut Forces.

With an Introduction and some Explanatory Notes by the *Reverend Mr. Thomas Prince.*

Psal. xliv. 1 — 3. *We have heard with our Ears, O God, our Fathers have told us, what Work Thou didst in their Days, in the times of old; How Thou didst drive out the Heathen with thy Hand, and plantedst Them: how Thou did afflict the People and cast them out. For they got not the Land in Possession by their own Sword, neither did their own Arm save them: but thy right Hand, and thine Ann, and the Light of thy Countenance, because Thou hadst a Favour unto them.*

Psal. cii. 18. *This shall be written for the Generation to come: and the People which shall be Created, shall praise the Lord.*

BOSTON:

Printed and Sold by *S. Kneeland* and *T. Green* in Queen Street, 1736.

Introduction

IN my Contemplations of the Divine Providence towards the People of New England, I have often tho't what a special Favour it was, that there came over with the first Settlers of Plimonth and Connecticut Colonies, which in those Times were especially exposed to the superiour Power of the Barbarians round about them; Two brave Englishmen bred to arms in the Dutch Netherlands, viz. Capt. Miles Standish of Plimouth, and Capt. John Mason of Connecticut: Gentlemen of tried Valour, Military Skill and Conduct, great Activity, and warm Zeal for that noble Cause of Pure Scriptural Religion, and Religious Liberty, which were the chief original Design and Interest of the Fathers of these Plantations; and who were acted with such eminent Degrees of Faith and Piety, as excited them to the most daring Enterprizes in the Cause of God and of his People, and went a great way to their wonderful Successes.

Like those inspired Heroes of whom we read the History in the Eleventh Chapter to the Hebrews— By Faith, they not only rather chose to suffer Affliction with the People of God than to enjoy the Pleasures of Sin for a Season; esteeming the Reproach of Christ greater Riches than the Treasures of Egypt: But by Faith they even forsook the same, passed thro' the Sea, subdued Kingdoms, wrought Righteousness, obtained Promises, waxed valiant in Fight, and turned to flight the armies of the Aliens.

The Judicious Reader that knows the New English History, cannot think these Scripture Phrases or religious Turns unsuitable on this Occasion: For as these Colonies were chiefly, if not entirely Settled by a Religious People, and for those Religious Purposes; It is as impossible to write an impartial or true History of them, as of the ancient Israelites, or the later Vaudois or North-Britons, without observing that Religious Spirit and Intention which evidently run through and animate their Historical Transactions.

Capt. Standish was of a low Stature, but of such a daring and active Genius, that even before the Arrival of the Massachusetts Colony, He spread a Terror over all the Tribes of Indians round about him, from the Massachusetts to Martha's Vineyard, and from Cape Cod Harbour to Narragansett. Capt. Mason was Tall and Portly, but never the less full of Martial Bravery and Vigour; that He soon became the equal Dread of the more numerous Nations from Narragansett to Hudson's River. They were Both the Instrumental Saviours of this Country in the most critical Conjunctures: And as we quietly enjoy the Fruits of their extraordinary Diligence and Valour, both the present and future Generations will for ever be obliged to revere their Memory.

Capt. Mason, the Writer of the following History, in which he was a principal Actor, as Chief Commander of the Connecticut Forces, is said to have been a Relative of Mr. John Mason the ancient Claimer of the Province of New-Hampshire: However, the Captain was one of the first who went up from the Massachusetts about the Year 1635 to lay the Foundation of Connecticut Colony: He went from Dorchester, first settled at Windsor, 1 and thence marched forth to the Pequot War.

But it being above Threescore Years since the following Narrative was Written, near an Hundred since the Events therein related, and the State of the New England Colonies being long since greatly Changed; it seems needful for the present Readers clearer Apprehension of these Matters, to Observe — That in the Year 1633, and 1634, several Englishmen arriving from England, at the Massachusetts, went up in the Western Country to discover Connecticut River; the next Year began to remove thither; and by the Beginning of 1637, Hartford, Windsor and Weathersfield were Settled, besides a Fortification built at Saybrook on the Mouth of the River.

At that Time there were especially three powerful and warlike Nations of Indians in the South Western Parts of New England; which spread all the Country from Aquethneck, since called Rhode Island, to Quinnepiack, since called New-Haven; viz. the Narragansetts, Pequots and Mohegans. The Narragansetts reached from the Bay of the same Name, to Pawcatuck River, now the Boundary between the Governments of Rhode Island and Connecticut: And their Head Sachem was Miantonimo. The Pequots reached from thence Westward to Connecticut River, and over it, as far as Branford, if not Quinnepiack; their Head Sachem being Sassacus. And the Mohegans spread along from the Narragansetts through the Inland Country, on the Back or Northerly Side of the Pequots, between them and the Nipmucks; their Head Sachem being Uncas.

The most terrible of all those Nations were then the Pequots; who with their depending Tribes soon entered on a Resolution to Destroy the English out of the Country. In 1634, they killed Capt. Stone and all his Company, being seven besides Himself, in and near his Bark on Connecticut River. In 1635, they killed Capt. Oldham in his Bark at Block-Island; and at Long-Island they killed two more cast away there. In 1636, and the following Winter and March, they killed six and took seven more at Connecticut River: Those they took alive they tortured to Death in a most barbarous Manner. And on April 23. 1637, they killed nine more and carried two young Women Captive at Weathersfield.

They had earnestly solicited the Narragansetts to engage in their Confederacy: very politickly representing to them, That if they should help or suffer the English to subdue the Pequots, they would thereby make Way for their own future Ruin; and that they need not come to open Battle with the English; only Fire our Houses, kill our Cattle, lye in Ambush and shoot us as we went about our Business; so we should be quickly forced to leave this Country, and the Indians not exposed to any great Hazard. Those truly politick Arguments were upon the Point of prevailing on the Narragansetts: And had

These with the Mohegans, to whom the Pequots were nearly related, joined against us; they might then, in the infant State of these Colonies, have easily accomplished their desperate Resolutions. But the Narragansetts being more afraid of the Pequots than of the English; were willing they should weaken each other, not in the least imagining the English could destroy them; at the same time an Agency from the Massachusetts Colony to the Narragansetts, happily Preserved their staggering Friendship. [2] And as Uncas the Great Sachim of the Moheags, upon the first coming of the English, fell into an intimate Acquaintance with Capt. Mason, He from the Beginning entertained us in an amicable Manner: And though both by his Father and Mother He derived from the Royal Blood of the Pequots, and had Married the Daughter of Tatobam their then late Sachim; yet such was his Affection for us, as he faithfully adhered to us, ventured his Life in our Service, assisted at the Taking their Fort, when about Seven Hundred of them were Destroyed, and thereupon in subduing and driving out of the Country the remaining greater Part of that fierce and dangerous Nation.

Soon after the War, Capt. Mason was by the Government of Connecticut, made the major General of all their forces, and so continued to the day of his death: The Rev. Mr. Hooker of Hartford, being desired by the Government in their Name to deliver the Staff into his Hand; We may imagine he did it with that superior Piety, Spirit and Majesty, which were peculiar to him: Like an ancient Prophet addressing himself to the Military Officer, delivering to him the Principal Ensign of Martial Power, to Lead the Armies and Fight the Battles of the Lord and of his People.

Major Mason having been trained up in the Netherland War under Sir Thomas Fairfax; [3] when the Struggle arose in England between K. Charles I. and the Parliament about the Royal Powers and the National Liberties; that Famous General had such an esteem for the Major's Conduct and Bravery, that He wrote to the Major to come over and help Him. [4] But the Major excusing himself, continued in this Country as long as he lived, and had some of the greatest Honours his Colony could yield him.

For besides his Office of Major General, the Colony in May 1660 chose him their Deputy Governour; continued him in the same Post by annual Re-elections, by virtue of their first Constitution to 1662 inclusively. The same Year K. Charles II. comprehending the Colonies of Connecticut and New Haven in One Government by the name of Connecticut Colony; He in the Royal Charter, signed April 23. appointed Major Mason their first Deputy Governour till the second Thursday of October following: After which, the General Court being left to chuse their Officers, they continued to chuse him their Deputy Governour every Year to May 1670; when his Age and Bodily Infirmities advancing, he laid down his Office and retired from Publick Business.

After the Pequot War, he had removed from Windsor to Saybrook: But in 1659, he removed thence to Norwich; where he Died in 1672, or 1673, in the

73d Year of his Age: leaving three sons, viz. Samuel, John and Daniel, to imi-
tate their Fathers Example and inherit his Virtues.

I have only now to observe, that in The Relation of the Troubles which
happened to New England by the Indians from 1614 to 1675, Published by
the then Mr. Increase Mather in 1677, I find a copy of the following Narrative,
but without the Prefaces, had been communicated to him by Mr. John Allyn
then the Secretary of Connecticut Colony; which that Rev. Author took for Mr.
Allyn' s and calls it his. But we must inform the Reader, that the Narrative
was originally drawn by Major Mason. And as his Eldest Grandson Capt. John
Mason now of New London has put it into my Hands; I have been more than
usually careful in Correcting the Press according to the Original; as the most
authentick Account of the Pequot War, and as a standing Monument both of
the extraordinary Dangers and Courage of our pious Fathers, and of the eminent Appearance of Heaven to save them. '

The other actions of Major Mason must be referred to the General History
of this country, when some Gentleman of greater Qualifications and Leisure
than I may claim, shall rise up among us, to undertake it. I shall give some
Hints in my Brief Chronology; which through numerous Hindrances, is now
in such a Forwardness that near 200 Pages are Printed al' ready; and in a
little Time, Life and Health allowed, I hope to present the Publick with the
first of the two ' intended Volumes. In the mean while I cannot but ' Regret it,
that such considerable and ancient Towns as Saybrook, Fairfield, Stamford,
Canterbury, Groton ' in the County of Middlesex, Chelmsford, Billerica, ' Wo-
burn, Dunstable and Bristol, should afford no ' more than their bare Names
in the Published Records of this Country.

Thomas Prince.

Boston, Dec. 23, 1735.

[1] The names of those who are known to have gone from Windsor are as follows: Capt. John Mason, Sergt. Benedict Alvord, Thomas Barber, Thomas Buck-
land, George Chappel, John Dyer, James Eggleston, Nathan Gillet, Thomas Gridley,
Thomas Stiles, Sergt. Thomas Staires, Richard Osborn, Thomas Parsons, William
Thrall. They were absent three weeks and two days. Every soldier received is. 1s
6d. per day, reckoning six days in the week; sergeants, 20d. per day; lieutenants,
20s. per week; the captain, 40s. per week. — Stiles' History of Ancient Windsor.
[2] The proposed Indian league was prevented by the diplomacy of Roger Williams. For, though he had been banished by the colony of Massachusetts, the
magistrates sought his counsel, which he gave freely, and was thus able to render
the infant colonies a service which proved to be of the greatest importance. In a
letter to John Mason in 1670, when both were old men, he writes as follows:
"When, the next year after my banishment, the Lord drew the bow of the Pequot
war against the country . . . . the Lord helped me immediately to put my life in my

19

hand, and scarce acquainting my wife, to ship myself all alone in a poor canoe, and to cut through a stormy wind with great seas, every minute in hazard of my life, to the sachem's house. Three days and nights my business forced me to lodge and mix with the bloody Pequot ambassadors, whose hands and arms reeked with the blood of my countrymen, murdered and massacred by them on Connecticut River, and from whom I could not but nightly look for their bloody knives at my own throat also."

[3] Fairfax went to the Netherlands in April of 1630, and though but eighteen, was a volunteer in the army and was with Sir Horace Vere at the siege of Bois-le-Duc, which surrendered in July of that year. Young Fairfax was then ordered by his grandfather to leave camp and travel in France; and there he remained for about eighteen months, returning to England in February of 1632. Since the total service of Fairfax in the Low Countries extended over but four months, and was somewhat in the nature of a youthful adventure, it can hardly be said that Mason was " trained up " under him, though the story has been repeated by nearly every biographer of Mason since Prince. He may, however, have been a companion in arms with Fairfax, though of this there is no direct proof.

[4] This statement by Prince seems to have been also without authority. However, Fairfax, who was no doubt the ablest general of the Civil War and a great organizer, must have known of the service of Captain Mason, and his " esteem " may have led him to write Mason in Connecticut to join Cromwell's army.

To the Honourable the General Court of Connecticut

Honoured Gentlemen,

You well know how often I have been requested by yourselves to write something in reference to the Subject of the ensuing Treatise (who have power to Command) and how backward I have been, as being conscious to my own unfitness; accounting it not so proper, I being a Chief Actor therein myself. Yet considering that little hath been done to keep the memory of such a special Providence alive, though I could heartily have wished that some other who had been less interested and better qualified might have undertaken the Task, for I am not unacquainted with my own Weakness; yet I shall endeavour in plainness and faithfulness impartially to declare the Matter, not taking the Crown from the Head of one and putting it upon another. There are several who have Wrote and also Printed at random on this Subject, greatly missing the Mark in many Things as I conceive. [5] I shall not exempt my self from frailties, yet from material Faults I presume you may pronounce it not Guilty, and do assure you that if I should see or by any be convinced of an Error, I shall at once confess and amend it. I thought it my Duty in the Entrance to relate the first Grounds upon which the English took up Anns against the Pequots; for the Beginning is the Moiety of the Whole; and not to mention some Passages at Rovers, as others have done, and not demonstrate the Cause. Judge of me as you please; I shall not climb after Applause, nor do I much fear a Censure; there being many Testimonies to what I shall say. 'Tis possible some may think no better can be expected in these distracting Times; it being so hard to please a few, impossible to please all: I shall therefore content myself that I have attended my rule: You may please to improve some others who were Actors in the Service to give in their Apprehensions, that so the severals being compared, you may enlarge or diminish as you shall see meet. I desire my Name may be sparingly mentioned: My principal Aim is that God may have his due praise.

By your unworthy Servant,

John Mason.

[5] Mason refers, no doubt, to the accounts by Underhill and Vincent, which had then been printed.

To the American Reader

To the Judicious Reader

Gentlemen,

I never had thought that this should have come to the Press, until of late: If I had, I should have endeavoured to have put a little more Varnish upon it: But being over perswaded by some Friends, I thought it not altogether amiss to present it to your courteous Disposition, hoping it might find your favourable Entertainment and Acceptance, though rude and impolished. I wish it had fallen into some better Hands that might have performed it to the life; I shall only draw the Curtain and open my little Casement, that so others of larger Hearts and Abilities may let in a bigger Light; that so at least some small Glimmering may be left to Posterity what Difficulties and Obstructions their Forefathers met with in their first settling these desart Parts of America; how God was pleased to prove them, and how by his wise Providence he ordered and disposed all their Occasions and Affairs for them in regard to both their Civils and Ecclesiasticals.

This with some other Reasons have been Motives to excite me to the enterprizing hereof; no man that I know of having as yet undertaken to write a general History or Relation; so that there is no Commemoration of Matters respecting this War; how they began, how carryed on, and continued, nor what Success they had. [1] They which think the mentioning of some Particulars is sufficient for the understanding of the General, in my Opinion stray no less from the Truth, than if by the separated Parts of a living Man one should think by this Means he knew all the Parts and Perfections of the Creature: But these separated Parts being joyned together having Form and Life, one might easily discern that he was deceived.

If the Beginning be but obscure, and the Ground uncertain, its Continuance can hardly perswade to purchase belief: Or if Truth be wanting in History, it proves but a fruitless Discourse.

I shall therefore, God helping, endeavour not so much to stir up the Affections of Men, as to declare in Truth and Plainness the Actions and Doings of Men; I shall therefore set down Matter in order as they Began and were carried on and Issued; that so I may not deceive the Reader in confounding of Things, but the Discourse may be both Plain and Easy.

And although some may think they have Wrote in a high Stile, and done some notable Thing, yet in my Opinion they have not spoken truly in some Particulars, and in general to little Purpose: For how can History find Credit, if in the Beginning you do not deliver plainly and clearly from whence and how you do come to the Relation which you presently intend to make of Actions?

As a Rule, although it hath less length and breadth, yet notwithstanding it retains the Name if it hath that which is proper to a Rule. When the Bones are Separated from a living Creature, it becomes unserviceable: So a History, if you take away Order and Truth, the rest will prove to be but a vain Narration.

I shall not make a long Discourse, nor labour to hold the Reader in doubt, using a multitude of Words, which is no sure Way to find out the Truth; as if one should seek for Verity in the Current of Pratling, having nothing but a conceit worthy to hold the Reader is suspence: (Sed quo vado) In a word, the

Lord was as it were pleased to say unto us, The Land of Canaan will I give unto thee though but few and Strangers in it: And when we went from one Nation to another, yea from one Kingdom to another, he suffered no Man to do us Wrong, but reproved Kings for our sakes: And so through Mercy at length we were settled in Peace, to the Astonishment of all that were round about us: unto whom be ascribed all Glory and Praise for ever and ever.

Farewell

John Mason.

Norwich, in New England, in America.

[1] The Author Died before the Reverend Mr. William Hubbard and Mr. Increase Mather Published their accounts of the Pequot War.

Some Grounds of the War Against the Pequots

About the Year 1632 one Capt. Stone arrived in the Massachusetts in a Ship from Virginia; who shortly after was bound for Virginia in a small Bark with one Capt. Norton; who sailing into Connecticut River about two Leagues from the Entrance cast Anchor; there coming to them several Indians belonging to that Place whom the Pequots Tyrannized over, being a potent and warlike People, it being their Custom so to deal with their neighbour Indians; Capt. Stone having some occasion with the Dutch who lived at a trading House near twenty Leagues up the River, procured some of those Indians to go as Pilots with two of his Men to the Dutch: But being benighted before they could come to their desired Port, put the skiff in which they went, ashoar, where the two Englishmen falling asleep, were both Murdered by their Indian Guides: There remaining with the Bark about twelve of the aforesaid Indians; who had in all probability formerly plotted their bloody Design; and waiting an opportunity when some of the English were on Shoar and Capt. Stone asleep in his Cabbin, set upon them and cruelly Murdered every one of them, plundered what they pleased and sunk the Bark.

These Indians were not native Pequots, but had frequent recourse unto them, to whom they tendered some of those Goods, which were accepted by the Chief Sachem of the Pequots: Other of the said Goods were tendered to Nynigrett Sachem of Nayanticke, who also received them.

The Council of the Massachusetts being informed of their proceedings, sent to speak with the Pequots, and had some Treaties with them: But being unsatisfied therewith, sent forth Captain John Endioot Commander in Chief, with Captain Underhill, Captain Turner, and with them one hundred and twenty Men: who were firstly designed on a Service against a People living on Block Island, who were subject to the Narragansett Sachem; they having taken a Bark of one Mr. John Oldham, Murdering him and all his Company: They were also to call the Pequots to an Account about the Murder of Capt,

Stone; who arriving at Pequot had some Conference with them; but little effected; only one Indian slain and some Wigwams burnt. After which, the Pequots grew inraged against the English who inhabited Connecticut, being but a small Number, about two hundred and fifty, who were there newly arrived; as also about twenty Men at Saybrook, under the Command of Lieutenant Lyon Gardner, who was there settled by several Lords and Gentlemen in England. The Pequots falling violently upon them, slew divers Men at Saybrook; keeping almost a constant Siege upon the Place; so that the English were constrained to keep within their pallizado Fort; being so hard Beset and sometimes Assaulted, that Capt. John Mason was sent by Connecticut Colony with twenty Men out of their small Numbers to secure the Place: But after his coming, there did not one Pequot appear in view for one Month Space, which was the time he there remained.

In the Interim certain Pequots about One Hundred going to a Place called Weathersfield on Connecticut; having formerly confederated with the Indians of that Place (as it was generally thought) lay in Ambush for the English; divers of them going into a large Field adjoining to the Town to their Labour, were there set upon by the Indians: Nine of the English were killed outright, with some Horses, and two young Women taken Captives.

At their Return from Weathersfield, they came down the River of Connecticut (Capt. Mason being then at Saybrook Fort) in three Canoes with about one hundred Men, which River of necessity they must pass: We espying them, concluded they had been acting some Mischief against us, made a Shot at them with a Piece of Ordnance, which beat off the Beak Head of one of their Canoes, wherein our two Captives were: it was at a very great distance: They then hastened, drew their Canoes over a narrow Beach with all speed and so got away.

Upon which the English were somewhat dejected: But immediately upon this, a Court was called and met in Hartford the First of May, 1637, [1] who seriously considering their Condition, which did look very Sad, for those Pequots were a great People, being strongly fortified, cruel, warlike, munitioned, &c. and the English but an handful in comparison: But their outrageous Violence against the English, having Murdered about Thirty of them, their great Pride and Insolency, constant pursuit in their malicious Courses, with their engaging other Indians in their Quarrel against the English, who had never offered them the least Wrong; who had in all likelihood Espoused all the Indians in the Country in their Quarrel, had not God by more than an ordinary Providence prevented: These Things being duly considered, witli the eminent Hazard and great Peril they were in; it pleased God so to stir up the Hearts of all Men in general, and the Court in special, that they concluded some Forces should forthwith be sent out against the Pequots; their Grounds being Just, and necessity enforcing them to engage in an offensive and defensive War; the Management of which War we are nextly to relate.

[1] May 1, 1637, was Monday.

25

An Epitome or brief History of the Pequot War

In the Beginning of May 1637 there were sent out by Connecticut Colony Ninety Men under the Command of Capt. John Mason against the Pequots, with Onkos an Indian Sachem living at Mohegan, [1] who was newly revolted from the Pequots; being Shipped in one Pink, one Pinnace, and one Shallop; who sailing down the River of Connecticut fell several times a ground, the Water being very low: The Indians not being wonted to such Things with their small Canoes, and also being impatient of Delays, desired they might be set on Shoar, promising that they would meet us at Saybrook; which we granted: They hastening to their Quarters, fell upon Thirty or forty of the Enemy near Saybrook Fort, and killed seven of them outright; [2] having only one of their' s wounded, who was sent back to Connecticut in a Skiff: Capt. John Underhill also coming with him, who informed us what was performed by Onkos and his Men; which we looked at as a special Providence; for before we were somewhat doubtful of his Fidelity: Capt. Underhill then offered his Service with nineteen Men to go with us, if Lieutenant Gardner would allow of it, who was Chief Commander at Saybrook Fort; which was readily approved of by Lieutenant Gardner and accepted by us; In lieu of them we sent back twenty of our Soldiers to Connecticut.

Upon a Wednesday we arrived at Saybrook, where we lay Windbound until Friday; often consulting how and in what manner we should proceed in our Enterprize, being altogether ignorant of the Country. At length we concluded, God assisting us, for Narragansett, and so to March through their Country, which Bordered upon the Enemy; where lived a great People, it being about fifteen Leagues beyond Pequot; The Grounds and Reasons of our so Acting you shall presently understand:

'First, The Pequots our Enemies, kept a continual ' Guard upon the River Night and Day.

'Secondly, their Numbers far exceeded ours; having sixteen Guns with Powder and Shot, as we were informed by the two Captives forementioned (where we declared the Grounds of this War) who were taken by the Dutch and restored to us at Saybrook; which indeed was a very friendly Office and not to be for' gotten.

'Thirdly, They were on Land, and being swift on Foot, might much impede our Landing, and possibly dishearten our Men; we being expected only by Land, ' there being no other Place to go on Shoar but in that River, nearer than Narragansett.

'Fourthly, By Narragansett we should come upon their Backs, and possibly might surprize them un' awares, at worst we should be on firm Land as well 'as they.' All which proved very successful as the Sequel may evidently demonstrate.

But yet for all this our Counsel, all of them except the Captain, were at a stand, and could not judge it meet to sail to Narragansett: And indeed there was a strong Ground for it; our Commission limiting us to land our Men in Pequot River; we had also the same Order by a Letter of Instruction sent us to Saybrook.

But Capt. Mason apprehending an exceeding great Hazard in so doing, for the Reasons forementioned, as also some other which I shall forbear to trouble you with, did therefore earnestly desire Mr. Stone that he would commend our Condition to the Lord, that Night, to direct how and in what manner we should demean ourselves in that Respect: He being our Chaplain and lying aboard our Pink, the Captain on Shoar. In the Morning very early Mr. Stone came ashoar to the Captain's Chamber, and told him, he had done as he had desired, and was fully satisfied to sail for Narragansett. [3] Our Council was then called, and the several Reasons alledged: In fine we all agreed with one accord to sail for Narragansett, which the next Morning we put in Execution.

I declare not this to encourage any Soldiers to Act beyond their Commission, or contrary to it; for in so doing they run a double Hazard. There was a great Commander in Belgia who did the States great Service in taking a City; but by going beyond his Commission lost his Life: His name was Grubbendunk. But if a War be Managed duly by Judgment and Discretion as is requisite, the Shews are many times contrary to what they seem to pursue: Whereof the more an Enterprize is dissembled and kept secret, the more facil to put in Execution; as the Proverb, The farthest way about is sometimes the nearest way home. I shall make bold to present this as my present Thoughts in this Case; In Matters of War, those who are both able and faithful should be improved; and then bind them not up into too narrow a Compass: For it is not possible for the wisest and ablest Senator to foresee all Accidents and Occurrents that fall out in the Management and Pursuit of a War: Nay although possibly he might be trained up in Military Affaires; and truly much less can he have any great Knowledge who hath had but little Experience therein. What shall I say? God led his People through many Difficulties and Turnings; yet by more than an ordinary Hand of Providence he brought them to Canaan at last.

On Friday Morning we set Sail for Narragansett Bay, and on Saturday towards Evening we arrived at our desired Port, there we kept the Sabbath.

On the Monday the Wind blew so hard at North West that we could not go on Shoar; as also on the Tuesday until Sun set; at which time Capt. Mason landed and Marched up to the Place of the Chief Sachem's Residence; who told the Sachem, 'That we had not an opportunity to acquaint him with our 1 coming Armed in his Country sooner; yet not doubting but it would be well accepted by him, there being Love betwixt himself and us; well knowing also that the Pequots and themselves were Enemies, and that he could not be unacquainted with those intolerable ' Wrongs and Injuries these Pequots had lately done unto the English; and that we were now come, God ' assisting, to Avenge our selves upon them; and that we did only desire free Passage through his Country.' Who returned us this Answer, That he did accept of our coming, and did also approve of our Design; only he thought our Numbers were too weak to deal with the Enemy, who were (as he said) very great Captains and Men skilful in War.' Thus he spake somewhat slighting of us.

On the Wednesday Morning, we Marched from thence to a Place called Nayanticke, it being about eighteen or twenty miles distant, where another of those Narragansett Sachems lived in a Fort; it being a Frontier to the Pequots. They carryed very proudly towards us; not permitting any of us to come into their Fort.

We beholding their Carriage and the Falsehood of Indians, and fearing least they might discover us to the Enemy, especially they having many times some of their near Relations among their greatest Foes; we therefore caused a strong Guard to be set about their Fort, giving Charge that no Indian should be suffered to pass in or out: We also informed the Indians, that none of them should stir out of the Fort upon peril of their Lives: so as they would not suffer any of us to come into their Fort, so we would not suffer any of them to go out of the Fort.

There we quartered that Night, the Indians not offering to stir out all the while.

In the Morning there came to us several of Miantomo [4] his Men, who told us, they were come to assist us in our Expedition, which encouraged divers Indians of that Place to Engage also; who suddenly gathering into a Ring, one by one, making solemn Protestations how galliantly they would demean themselves, and how many Men they would Kill.

On the Thursday about eight of the Clock in the Morning, we Marched thence towards Pequot, with about five hundred Indians: But through the Heat of the Weather and want of Provisions some of our Men fainted: And having Marched about twelve Miles, we came to Pawcatuck River, at a Ford where our Indians told us the Pequots did usually Fish; there making an Alta, we stayed some small time: The Narragansett Indians manifesting great Fear, in so much that many of them returned, although they had frequently despised us, saying, That we durst not look upon a Pequot, but themselves would perform great Things; though we had often told them that we came on purpose and were resolved, God assisting, to see the Pequots, and to fight with them, before we returned, though we perished. I then enquired of Onkos, what he thought the Indians would do? Who said, The Narragansetts would all leave us, but as for Himself He would never leave us: and so it proved: For which Expressions and some other Speeches of his, I shall never forget him. Indeed he was a great Friend, and did great Service.

And after we had refreshed our selves with our mean Commons, we Marched about three Miles, and came to a Field which had lately been planted with Indian Corn: There we made another Alt, and called our Council, supposing we drew near to the Enemy: and being informed by the Indians that the Enemy had two Forts almost impregnable; but we were not at all Discouraged, but rather Animated, in so much that we were resolved to Assault both their Forts at once. But understanding that one of them was so remote that we could not come up with it before Midnight, though we Marched hard; whereat we were much grieved, chiefly because the greatest and bloodiest Sachem there resided, whose name was Sassacous: We were then constrained, being exceedingly spent in our March with extream Heat and want of Necessaries, to accept of the nearest.

We then Marching on in a silent Manner, the Indians that remained fell all into the Rear, who formerly kept the Van; (being possessed with great Fear) we continued our March till about one Hour in the Night: and coming to a little Swamp between two Hills, there we pitched our little Camp; much wearied with hard Travel, keeping great Silence, supposing we were very near the Fort; as our Indians informed us; which proved otherwise: The Rocks were our Pillows; yet Rest was pleasant: The Night proved Comfortable, being clear and Moon Light: We appointed our Guards and placed our Sentinels at some distance; who heard the Enemy Singing at the Fort, who continued that Strain until Midnight, with great Insulting and Rejoycing, as we were afterwards informed: They seeing our Pinnaces sail by them some Days before, concluded we were afraid of them and durst not come near them; the Burthen of their Song tending to that purpose. In the Morning, we awaking and seeing it very light, supposing it had been day, and so we might have lost our Opportunity, having purposed to make our mason's narrative. 27 Assault before Day; rowsed the Men with all expedition, and briefly commended ourselves and Design to God, thinking immediately to go to the Assault; the Indians shewing us a Path, told us that it led directly to the Fort. We held on our March about two Miles, wondering that we came not to the Fort, and fearing we might be deluded: But seeing Corn newly planted at the Foot of a great Hill, supposing the Fort was not far off, a Champion Country being round about us; then making a stand, gave the Word for some of the Indians to come up: At length Onkos and one Wequash appeared; We demanded of them, Where was the Fort? They answered On the Top of that Hill: Then we demanded, Where were the Rest of the Indians? They answered, Behind, exceedingly afraid: We wished them to tell the rest of their Fellows, That they should by no means Fly, but stand at what distance they pleased, and see whether English Men would now Fight or not. Then Capt. Underhill came up, who Marched in the Rear; and commending ourselves to God, divided our Men: There being two Entrances into the Fort, intending to enter both at once: Captain Mason leading up to that on the North East Side; who approaching within one Rod, heard a Dog bark and an Indian crying Owanux!

Owanux! which is Englishmen! Englishmen! We called up our Forces with all expedition, gave Fire upon them through the Pallizado; the Indians being in a dead indeed their last Sleep: Then we wheeling off fell upon the main Entrance, which was blocked up with Bushes about Breast high, over which the Captain passed, intending to make good the Entrance, encouraging the rest to follow. Lieutenant Seeley endeavoured to enter; but being somewhat cumbred, stepped back and pulled out the Bushes and so entred, and with him about sixteen Men: We had formerly concluded to destroy them by the Sword and save the Plunder.

Whereupon Captain Mason seeing no Indians, entred a Wigwam; where he was beset with many Indians, waiting all opportunities to lay Hands on him, but could not prevail. At length William Heydon [5] espying the Breach in the Wigwam, supposing some English might be there, entred; but in his Entrance fell over a dead Indian; but speedily recovering himself, the Indians some fled, others crept under their Beds: The Captain going out of the Wigwam saw many Indians in the Lane or Street; he making towards them, they fled, were pursued to the End of the Lane, where they were met by Edward Pattison, Thomas Barber, with some others; where seven of them were Slain, as they said. The Captain facing about, Marched a slow Pace up the Lane he came down, perceiving himself very much out of Breath; and coming to the other End near the Place where he first entred, saw two Soldiers standing close to the Pallizado with their Swords pointed to the Ground: The Captain told them that We should never kill them after that manner: The Captain also said, We must Burn them; and immediately stepping into the Wigwam where he had been before, brought out a Firebrand, and putting it into the Matts with which they were covered, set the Wigwams on Fire. Lieutenant Thomas Bull and Nicholas Omsted beholding, came up; and when it was thoroughly kindled, the Indians ran as Men most dreadfully Amazed.

And indeed such a dreadful Terror did the Almighty let fall upon their Spirits, that they would fly from us and run into the very Flames, where many of them perished. And when the Fort was thoroughly Fired, Command was given, that all should fall off and surround the Fort; which was readily attended by all; only one Arthur Smith being so wounded that he could not move out of the Place, who was happily espied by Lieutenant Bull, and by him rescued.

The Fire was kindled on the North East Side to windward; which did swiftly over-run the Fort, to the extream Amazement of the Enemy, and great Rejoycing of our selves. Some of them climbing to the Top of the Pallizado; others of them running into the very Flames; many of them gathering to windward, lay pelting at us with their Arrows; and we repayed them with our small Shot: Others of the Stoutest issued forth, as we did guess, to the Number of Forty, who perished by the Sword.

What I have formerly said, is according to my own Knowledge, there being sufficient living Testimony to every Particular.

But in reference to Captain Underhill and his Parties acting in this Assault, I can only intimate as we were informed by some of themselves immediately after the Fight, Thus They Marching up to the Entrance on the South West Side, there made some Pause; a valiant, resolute Gentleman, one Mr. Hedge, stepping towards the Gate, saying, If We may not Enter, wherefore came we here; and immediately endeavoured to Enter; but was opposed by a sturdy Indian which did impede his Entrance; but the Indian being slain by himself and Sergeant Davis, Mr. Hedge Entred the Fort with some others; but the Fort being on Fire, the Smoak and Flames were so violent that they were constrained to desert the Fort.

Thus were they now at their Wits End, who not many Hours before exalted themselves in their great Pride, threatning and resolving the utter Ruin and Destruction of all the English, Exulting and Rejoycing with Songs and Dances: But God was above them, who laughed his Enemies and the Enemies of his People to Scorn, making them as a fiery Oven: Thus were the Stout Hearted spoiled, having slept their last Sleep, and none of their Men could find their Hands: Thus did the Lord judge among the Heathen, filling the Place with dead Bodies!

And here we may see the just Judgment of God, in sending even the very Night before this Assault, One hundred and fifty Men from their other Fort, to join with them of that Place, who were designed as some of themselves reported to go forth against the English, at that very Instant when this heavy Stroak came upon them where they perished with their Fellows. So that the Mischief they intended to us, came upon their own Pate: They were taken in their own snare, and we through Mercy escaped. And thus in little more than one Hour's space was their impregnable Fort with themselves utterly Destroyed, to the Number of six or seven Hundred, as some of themselves confessed. There were only seven taken captive, and about seven escaped. [6]

Of the English, there were two Slain outright, and about twenty Wounded: Some Fainted by reason of the sharpness of the Weather, it being a cool Morning, and the want of such Comforts and Necessaries as were needful in such a Case; especially our Chyrurgeon [7] was much wanting, whom we left with our Barks in Narragansett Bay, who had Order there to remain until the Night before our intended Assault.

And thereupon grew many Difficulties: Our Provision and Munition near spent; we in the enemies Country, who did far exceed us in Number, being much enraged: all our Indians, except Onkos, deserting us; our Pinnaces at a great distance from us, and when they would come we were uncertain.

But as we were consulting what Course to take, it pleased God to discover our Vessels to us before a fair Gale of Wind, sailing into Pequot Harbour, to our great Rejoycing.

We had no sooner discovered our Vessels, but immediately came up the Enemy from the other Fort; Three Hundred or more as we conceived. The Captain lead out a file or two of Men to Skirmish with them, chiefly to try what temper they were of, who put them to a stand: we being much encouraged thereat, presently prepared to March towards our Vessels: Four or Five of our Men were so wounded that they must be carried with the Arms of twenty more. We also being faint, were constrained to put four to one Man, with the Arms of the rest that were wounded to others; so that we had not above forty Men free: at length we hired several Indians, who eased us of that Burthen, in carrying of our wounded Men. And Marching about one quarter of a Mile; the Enemy coming up to the Place where the Fort was, and beholding what was done, stamped and tore the Hair from their Heads: And after a little space, came mounting down the Hill upon us, in a full career, as if they would over run us; But when they came within Shot, the Rear faced about, giving Fire upon them: Some of them being Shot, made the rest more wary: Yet they held on running to and fro, and shooting their Arrows at Random. There was at the Foot of the Hill a small Brook, where we rested and refreshed our selves, having by that time taught them a little more Manners than to disturb us.

We then Marched on towards Pequot Harbour; and falling upon several Wigwams, burnt them: The Enemy still following us in the Rear, which was to windward, though to little purpose; yet some of them lay in Ambush behind Rocks and Trees, often shooting at us, yet through Mercy touched not one of us; And as we came to any Swamp or Thicket, we made some Shot to clear the Passage. Some of them fell with our Shot; and probably more might, but for want of Munition: But when any of them fell, our Indians would give a great Shout, and then would they take so much Courage as to fetch their Heads. And thus we continued, until we came within two Miles of Pequot Harbour; where the Enemy gathered together and left us; we Marching on to the Top of an Hill adjoining to the Harbour, with our Colours flying; having left our Drum at the Place of our Rendezvous the Night before: We seeing our Vessels there Riding at Anchor, to our great Rejoycing, and came to the Water-Side, we there sat down in Quiet.

Captain Patrick being Arrived there with our Vessels, who as we were informed was sent with Forty Men by the Massachusetts Colony, upon some Service against the Block Islanders; Who coming to the Shore in our Shallop with all his Company, as he said to Rescue us, supposing we were pursued, though there did not appear any the least sign of such a Thing.

But we could not prevail with Him by any Means to put his Men ashore, that so we might carry our Wounded Men a Board; although it was our own Boat in which he was: We were very much Troubled; but knew not how to help our selves. At length we were fetched a Board to the great Rejoycing of our Friends.

Shortly after our coming a Board, there fell out a great Contest between Captain Underhill and Capt. Patrick: Captain Underhill claiming an Interest in the Bark where Captain Patrick was, which indeed was Underhill's Right; The Contest grew to a great Height. At length we propounded, that if Patrick would Ride there with that Bark in Contention, and secure the Narragansett Indians, it being also the Place of Rendezvous to those Vessels that were expected from Massachuset, until we Transported our Wounded Men to Saybrook five Leagues distant; then we would immediately return our Pink to convey the Narragansetts home: The which Captain Patrick seemed very readily to accept.

Capt. Underhill soon after set sail in one of our Barks for Saybrook: But before he was out of Sight; Captain Patrick signified by Writing, that he could not attend that Service, but he must wait for the Bay Vessels at Saybrook, wishing us, having the Honour of that Service to compleat it, by securing the Narragansett Indians; which at first seemed very Difficult, if not Impossible: For our Pink could not receive them, and to march by Land was very Dangerous; it being near twenty Miles in the Enemies Country, our Numbers being much weakened, we were then about twenty Men; the rest we had sent home for fear of the Pequots Invasion. But absolutely neccesitated to March by Land, we hasted ashore, with our Indians and small Numbers. Captain Patrick seeing what we intended, came ashore also with his Men; although in truth we did not desire or delight in his Company, and so we plainly told him: However he would and did March a long with us.

About the midway between that and Saybrook, we fell upon a People called Nayanticks, belonging to the Pequots, who fled to a Swamp for Refuge: They hearing or espying of us, fled: we pursued them a while by the Track, as long as they kept together: But being much spent with former Travel, and the Sabbath drawing on, it being about Two or Three of the Clock on the Saturday in the Afternoon; we leaving our Pursuit, hasted towards Saybrook, about Sun set we Arrived at Connecticut River Side; being nobly Entertained by Lieutenant Gardner with many great Guns: But were forced there to Quarter that Night: On the Morrow we were all fetched over to Saybrook, receiving many Courtesies from Lieut. Gardner.

And when we had taken Order for the safe Conduct of the Narragansett Indians, we repaired to the Place of our Abode: where we were Entertained with great Triumph and Rejoycing and Praising God for his Goodness to us, in succeeding our weak Endeavours, in Crowning us with Success, and restoring of us with so little Loss. Thus was God seen in the Mount, Crushing his proud Enemies and the Enemies of his People: They who were ere while a Terror to all that were round about them, who resolved to Destroy all the English and to Root their very Name out of this Country, should by such weak Means, even Seventy seven (there being no more at the Fort) bring the Mischief they plotted, and the Violence they offered and exercised, upon their own Heads in a Moment: burning them up in the fire of his Wrath, and dunging the Ground with their Flesh: It was the Lord's Doings, and it is marvellous in our Eyes! It is He that hath made his Work wonderful, and therefore ought to be remembred.

Immediately the whole Body of Pequots repaired to that Fort where Sessacous the Chief Sachem did reside; charging him that he was the only Cause of all the Troubles that had befallen them; and therefore they would Destroy both him and his: But by the Intreaty of their Counsellors they spared his Life; and consulting what Course to take, concluded there was no abiding any longer in their Country, and so resolved to fly into several Parts. The greatest Body of them went towards Manhatance: [8] And passing over Connecticut, they met with three English Men in a Shallop going for Saybrook, whom they slew: The English Fought very stoutly, as themselves confessed, Wounding many of the Enemy.

About a Fortnight after our Return home, which was about one Month after the Fight at Mistick, there Arrived in Pequot River several Vessels from the Massachusetts, Captain Israel Stoughton being Commander in Chief; and with him about One hundred and twenty Men; being sent by that Colony to pursue the War against the Pequots: The Enemy being all fled before they came, except some few Straglers, who were surprised by the Moheags and others of the Indians, and by them delivered to the Massachusetts Soldiers.

Connecticut Colony being informed hereof, sent forthwith forty Men, Captain Mason being Chief Commander; with some other Gent, to meet those of the Massachusetts, to consider what was necessary to be attended respecting the future: Who meeting with them of the Massachusetts in Pequot Harbour; after some time of consultation, concluded to pursue those Pequots that were fled towards Manhatance, and so forthwith Marched after them, discovering several Places where they Rendezvoused and lodged not far distant from their several Removes; making but little haste, by reason of their Children, and want of Provision; being forced to dig for Clams, and to procure such other things as the Wilderness afforded: Our Vessels sailing along by the Shore. In about the space of three Days we all Arrived at New Haven Harbour, then called Quinnypiag. And seeing a great Smoak in the Woods not far distant, we supposing some of the Pequots our Enemies might be there; we hastened ashore, but quickly discovered them to be Connecticut Indians. Then we returned aboard our Vessels, where we stayed some short time, having sent a Pequot Captive upon discovery, we named him Luz; who brought us Tydings of the Enemy, which proved true: so faithful was he to us, though against his own Nation. Such was the Terror of the English upon them; that a Moheage Indian named Jack Eatow going ashore at that time, met with three Pequots, took two of them and brought them aboard.

We then hastened our march towards the Place where the Enemy was: And coming into a Corn Field, several of the English espyed some Indians, who fled from them: They pursued them; and coming to the Top of an Hill, saw several Wigwams just opposite, only a Swamp intervening, which was almost divided in two Parts. Sergeant Palmer hastening with about twelve Men who were under his Command to surround the smaller Part of the Swamp, that so He might prevent the Indians flying; Ensign Danport, [9] Sergeant Jeffries &c, entering the Swamp, intended to have gone to the Wigwams, were there set upon by several Indians, who in all probability were deterred by Sergeant Palmer. In this Skirmish the English slew but few; two or three of themselves were Wounded: The rest of the English coming up, the Swamp was surrounded.

Our Council being called, and the Question propounded, How we should proceed, Captain Patrick advised that we should cut down the Swamp; there being many Indian Hatchets taken, Captain Traske concurring with him; but was opposed by others: Then we must pallizado the Swamp; which was also opposed: Then they would have a Hedge made like those of Gotham; all which was judged by some almost impossible, and to no purpose, and that for several Reasons, and therefore strongly opposed. But some others advised to force the Swamp, having time enough, it being about three of the Clock in the Afternoon: But that being opposed, it was then propounded to draw up our Men close to the Swamp, which would much have lessened the Circumference; and with all to fill up the open Passages with Bushes, that so we might secure them until the Morning, and then we might consider further about it. But neither of these would pass; so different were our Apprehensions; which was very grievous to some of us, who concluded the Indians would make an Escape in the Night, as easily they might and did: We keeping at a great distance, what better could be expected? Yet Captain Mason took Order that the Narrow in the Swamp should be cut through; which did much shorten our Leaguer. It was resolutely performed by Serjeant Davis.

We being loth to destroy Women and Children, as also the Indians belonging to that Place; whereupon Mr. Tho. Stanton a Man well acquainted with Indian Language and Manners, offered his Service to go into the Swamp and treat with them: To which we were somewhat backward, by reason of some Hazard and Danger he might be exposed unto: But his importunity prevailed: Who going to them, did in a short time return to us, with near Two Hundred old Men, Women and Children; who delivered themselves, to the Mercy of the English. And so Night drawing on, we beleaguered them as strongly as we could. About half an Hour before Day, the Indians that were in the Swamp attempted to break through Captain Patrick's Quarters; but were beaten back several times; they making a great Noise, as their Manner is at such Times, it sounded round about our Leaguer: Whereupon Captain Mason sent Sergeant Stares to inquire into the Cause, and also to assist if need required; Capt. Traske coming also in to their Assistance: But the Tumult growings to a very great Height, we raised our Siege; and Marching up to the Place, at a Turning of the Swamp the Indians were forcing out upon us; but we sent them back by our small Shot.

We waiting a little for a second Attempt; the Indians in the mean time facing about, pressed violently upon Captain Patrick, breaking through his Quarters, and so escaped. They were about sixty or seventy as we were informed. We afterwards searched the Swamp, and found but few Slain. The

Captives we took were about One Hundred and Eighty; whom we divided, intending to keep them as Servants, but they could not endure that Yoke; few of them continuing any considerable time with their masters.

Thus did the Lord scatter his Enemies with his strong Ann! The Pequots now became a Prey to all Indians. Happy were they that could bring in their Heads to the English: Of which there came almost daily to Winsor, or Hartford. But the Pequots growing weary hereof, sent some of the Chief that survived to mediate with the English; offering that If they might but enjoy their Lives, they would become the English Vassals, to dispose of them as they pleased. Which was granted them. Whereupon Onkos and Myantonimo were sent for; who with the Pequots met at Hartford. The Pequots being demanded, how many of them were then living? Answered, about One Hundred and Eighty, or two Hundred. There were then given to Onkos, Sachem of Monheag, Eighty; to Myantonimo, Sachem of Narragansett, Eighty; and to Nynigrett, [10] Twenty, when he should satisfy for a Mare of Edward Pomroye's killed by his Men. The Pequots were then bound by Covenant, That none should inhabit their native Country, nor should any of them be called Pequots any more, but Moheags and Narragansetts forever. Shortly after, about Forty of them went to Moheag; others went to Long Island; the rest settled at Pawcatuck, a Place in Pequot Country, contrary to their late Covenant and Agreement with the English.

Which Connecticut taking into Consideration, and well weighing the several Inconveniences that might ensue; for the Prevention whereof, they sent out forty Men under the command of Captain John Mason, to supplant them, by burning their Wigwams, and bringing away their Corn, except they would desert the Place: Onkos with about One Hundred of his Men in twenty Canoes, going also to assist in the Service. As we sailed into Pawcatuck-Bay We met with three of those Indians, whom we sent to inform the rest with the end of our coming, and also that we desired to speak with some of them: They promised speedily to return us an Answer, but never came to us more.

We run our Vessel up into a small River, and by reason of Flatts were forced to land on the West Side; their Wigwams being on the East just opposite, where we could see the Indians running up and down Jeering of us. But we meeting with a narrow place in the River between two rocks, drew up our Indians Canoes, and got suddenly over sooner than we were expected or desired; Marching immediately up to their Wigwams; the Indians being all fled, except some old People that could not.

We were so suddenly upon them that they had not time to convey away their Goods: We viewed their Corn, whereof there was Plenty, it being their time of Harvest: And coming down to the Water Side to our Pinnace with half of Onkos' s his Men, the rest being plundering the Wigwams; we looking towards a Hill not far remote, we espyed about sixty Indians running towards us; we supposing they were our absent Men, the Moheags that were with us not speaking one word, nor moving towards them until the other came within thirty or forty paces of them; then they run and met them and fell on pell mell striking and cutting with Bows, Hatchets, Knives, &c. after their feeble Manner: Indeed it did hardly deserve the Name of Fighting. We then endeavoured to get between them and the Woods, that so we might prevent their flying; which they perceiving, endeavoured speedily to get off under the beach: we made no Shot at them, nor any hostile Attempt upon them. Only seven of them who were Nynigrett's Men, were taken. Some of them growing very outrageous, whom we intended to have made shorter by the Head; and being about to put it in Execution; one Otash a Sachem of Narragansett, Brother to Myantonimo stepping forth, told the Captain, They were his Brother's Men, and that he was a Friend to the English, and if he would spare their Lives we should have as many Murtherer's Heads in lieu of them which should be delivered to the English. We considering that there was no Blood shed as yet, and that it tended to Peace and Mercy, granted his Desire; and so delivered them to Onkos to secure them until his Engagement was performed, because our Prison had been very much pestered with such Creatures.

We then drew our Bark into a Creek, the better to defend her; for there were many Hundreds, within five Miles waiting upon us. There we Quartered that Night: In the Morning as soon as it was Light there appeared in Arms at least Three Hundred Indians on the other Side the Creek: Upon which we stood to our Anns; which they perceiving, some of them fled, others crept behind the Rocks and Trees, not one of them to be seen. We then called to them, saying, We desired to speak with them, and that we would down our Arms for that end: Whereupon they stood up: We then informed them, That the Pequots had violated their Promise with the English, in that they were not there to inhabit, and that we were sent to supplant them: They answered saying, The Pequots were good Men, their Friends, and they would Fight for them, and protect them: At which we were somewhat moved, and told them, It was not far to the Head of the Creek where we would meet them, and then they might try what they could do in that Respect.

They then replied, That they would not Fight with English Men, for they were Spirits, but would Fight with Onkos. We replyed, That we thought it was too early for them to Fight, but they might take their opportunity; we should be burning Wigwams, and carrying Corn aboard all that Day. And presently beating up our Drum, we Fired the Wigwams in their View: And as we Marched, there were two Indians standing upon a Hill jeering and reviling of us: Mr. Thomas Stanton our Interpreter, Marching at Liberty, desired to make a Shot at them; the Captain demanding of the Indians. What they were? Who said, They were Murtherers: Then the said Stanton having leave, let fly, Shot one of them through both his Thighs; which was to our Wonderment, it being at such a vast distance.

We then loaded our Bark with Corn; and our Indians their Canoes: And thirty more which we had taken, with Kittles, Trays, Mats, and other Indian

Luggage, That Night we went all aboard, and set Sail homeward: It pleased God in a short Time to bring us all in safety to the Place of our Abode; although we strook and stuck upon a Rock. The Way and Manner how God dealt with us in our Delivery was very Remarkable; The Story would be somewhat long to trouble you with at this time; and therefore I shall forbear.

Thus we may see, How the Face of God is set against them that do Evil, to cut off the Remembrance of them from the Earth. Our Tongue shall talk of thy Righteousness all the Day long; for they are confounded, they are brought to Shame that sought our Hurt! Blessed be the Lord God of Israel, who only doth wondrous Things; and blessed be his holy Name for ever: Let the whole Earth be filled with his Glory! Thus the Lord was pleased to smite our Enemies in the hinder Parts, and to give us their Land for an Inheritance: Who remembred us in our low Estate, and redeemed us out of our Enemies Hands: Let us therefore praise the Lord for his Goodness and his wonderful Works to the Children of Men!

[1] Onkos; usually called Uncas, the Great Sachem of the Moheags.
[2] Mr. Increase Mather, in his History of the Pequot War, says this was on May 15.
[3] Mr. J. H. Bromley, in his Oration on John Mason, suggests that "Mason, though a profoundly religious man, had the worldly wisdom to give to Mr. Stone such knowledge of the facts as to be able to lay them intelligently before the Lord."
[4] He was usually called Miantonimo the Great Sachem of the Narragansett Indians.
[5] Notwithstanding the statement by Trumbull and others, that Davis cut the bowstring and saved the life of Mason, there is reason, well supported by tradition, for believing that this service was performed by Heydon, and that the incident occurred at this very moment. It will be seen that Mason entered the fort on one side, and that Davis entered on the opposite with Captain Underhill, and could therefore not have been near. The sword of Heydon that is said to have cut the bowstring is in the possession of the Connecticut Historical Society.
[6] The place of the Fort being called Mistick, this Fight was called Mistick Fight: And Mr. Increase Mather, from a Manuscript he met with, tells us; It was on Friday, May 26. 1637, a memorable Day!
[7] This surgeon, whose name was Pell, had been attached to Saybrook Fort, and was sent on the expedition by Gardener.
[8] I suppose this the same which is sometimes called Manhatan or Manhatoes; which is since called New York.
[9] It should be Davenport, who was afterwards Captain of the Castle in Boston Harbour.
[10] He was usually called Ninnicraft.

Addition.

I shall add a Word or two by way of Coment.

Our Commons were very short, there being a general scarcity through-
out the Colony of all sorts of Provision, it being upon our first Arrival at the
Place. We had but one Pint of strong Liquors among us in our whole March,
but what the Wilderness afforded; (the Bottle of Liquor being in my Hand)
and when it was empty, the very smelling to the Bottle would presently re-
cover such as Fainted away, which happened by the extremity of the Heat:
And thus we Marched on in an uncoath and unknown Path to the English,
though much frequented by Indians. And was not the Finger mason's narrative. 45 of God in all this? By his special Providence to lead us along in the
Way we should go: Nay though we knew not where their Forts were, how far
it was to them, nor the Way that led to them, but by what we had from our
Indian Guides; whom we could not confide in, but looked at them as uncertain: And yet notwithstanding all our Doubts, we should be brought on the
very fittest Season; nay and which is yet more, that we should be carried in
our March among a treacherous and perfidious People, yea in our allodgment
so near the Enemy, all Night in so populous a Country, and not the least notice of us; seemeth somewhat strange, and more than ordinary: Nay that we
should come to their very Doors: What shall I say: God was pleased to hide us
in the Hollow of his Hand; I still remember a Speech of Mr. Hooker at our going aboard; That they should be Bread for us. And thus when the Lord turned
the Captivity of his People, and turned the Wheel upon their Enemies; we
were like Men in a Dream; then was our Mouth filled with Laughter, and our
Tongues with Singing; thus we may say the Lord hath done great Things for
us among the Heathen, whereof we are glad. Praise ye the Lord!

I shall mention two or three special Providences that God was pleased to
vouchsafe to Particular Men; viz. two Men, being one Man's Servants, namely,
John Dier and Thomas Stiles, were both of them Shot in the Knots of their
Handkerchiefs, being about their Necks, and received no Hurt. Lieutenant
Seeley was Shot in the Eyebrow with a flat headed Arrow, the Point turning
downwards: I pulled it out myself. Lieutenant Bull had an Arrow Shot into a
hard piece of Cheese, having no other Defence: Which may verify the old Say-
ing, A little Armour would serve if a Man knew where to place it. Many such
Providences happened; some respecting my self; but since there is none that
Witness to them, I shall forbear to mention them.

The Year ensuing, the Colony being in extream Want of Provision, many
giving twelve Shillings for one Bushel of Indian Corn; the Court of Connecticut imploying Captain Mason, Mr. William Wadsworth and Deacon Stebbin,
to try what Providence would afford, for their Belief in this great Straight:
Who notwithstanding some discouragement they met with from some Eng-

lish, went to a Place called Pocomtuck: [1] where they procured so much Corn at reasonable Bates, that the Indians brought down to Hartford and Windsor, Fifty Canoes laden with Corn at one time. Never was the like known to this Day! So although the Lord was pleased to shew his People hard Things; yet did he execute Judgment for the Oppressed, and gave Food to the Hungry. O let us meditate on the Great Works of God: Ascribing all Blessing and Praise to his Great Name, for all his Great Goodness and Salvation! Amen, Amen.

FINIS.

[1] Since called Deerfield.

Nevves From America;

OR,

A NEW AND EXPERIMENTAL DISCOVERIE OF
New England;
containing,
A TRVE RELATION OF THEIR
War-like proceedings these two yeares last
past, with a Figure of the Indian Fort,
or Palizado.

Also a discovery of these places, that as yet have very few or no Inhabitants, which would yeeld speciall accommodation to such as will Plant there:

Viz.
Queenapoick. Agu-wom. Hudson's River. Long Island. Nahanticut. Martins Vineyard. Pequet. Naransett Bay. Elizabeth Islands. Puscataway. Casko, with about a hundred Islands neere to Casko.

By Captaine Iohn Underhill, a Commander in the Warres there.

LONDON,
Printed by J. D. for *Peter Cole,* and are to be sold at the signe
of the Glove in Corne-hill neere
the Royall Exchange. 1638.

[Capt. John Underhill, the author of this History of the Pequot War, was one of the first planters of Massachusetts, one of the three first deputies from Boston to the General Court, and one of the earliest officers of the Ancient and Honorable Artillery Company. Further particulars of his chequered life and eccentric character may be found in Eliot's Biographical Dictionary, and more abundantly in Gov. Winthrop's History of New England.

The following Tract being exceedingly rare, only one copy being known to exist on this side of the Atlantic, belonging to the Library of Harvard University, it was thought desirable to perpetuate it by multiplying copies of it in our Historical Collections. * * * * *Publishing Committee, Mass. Hist. Soc*]

News from America, or a late and experimental discovery of New England

I shall not spend time (for my other occasions will not permit) to write largely of every particular, but shall, as briefly as I may, perform these two things; first, give a true narration of the warlike proceedings that hath been in New England these two years last past; secondly, I shall discover to the reader divers places in New England, that would afford special accommodations to such persons as will plant upon them. I had not time to do either of these as they deserved; but wanting time to do it as the nature of the thing required, I shall, according to my ability, begin with a relation of our warlike proceedings, and will interweave the special places fit for new plantations, with their description, as I shall find occasion, in the following discourse. But I shall, according to my promise, begin with a true relation of the New England wars against the Block Islanders, and that insolent and barbarous nation, called the Pequeats, whom, by the sword of the Lord, and a few feeble instruments, soldiers not accustomed to war, were drove out of their country, and slain by the sword, to the number of fifteen hundred souls, in the space of two months and less; so as their country is fully subdued and fallen into the hands of the English. And to the end that God's name might have the glory, and his people see his power, and magnify his honor for his great goodness, I have endeavored, according to my weak ability, to set forth the full relation of the war, from the first rise to the end of the victory.

The cause of our war against the Block Islanders, was for taking away the life of one Master John Oldham, who made it his common course to trade amongst the Indians. He coming to Block Island to drive trade with them, the islanders came into his boat, and having got a full view of commodities which gave them good content, consulted how they might destroy him and his company, to the end they might clothe their bloody flesh with his lawful garments. The Indians having laid the plot, into the boat they came to trade,

42

as they pretended; watching their opportunities, knocked him in the head, and martyred him most barbarously, to the great grief of his poor distressed servants, which by the providence of God were saved. This island lying in the road way to Lord Sey and the Lord Brooke's plantation, a certain seaman called to John Gallop, master of the small navigation standing along to the Mathethusis Bay, and seeing a boat under sail close aboard the island, and perceiving the sails to be unskilfully managed, bred in him a jealousy, whether that the island Indians had not bloodily taken the life of our countrymen, and made themselves master of their goods. Suspecting this, he bore up to them, and approaching near them was confirmed that his jealousy was just. Seeing Indians in the boat, and knowing her to be the vessel of Master Oldham, and not seeing him there, gave fire upon them and slew some; others leaped overboard, besides two of the number which he preserved alive and brought to the Bay. The blood of the innocent called for vengeance. God stirred up the heart of the honored Governor, Master Henry Vane, and the rest of the worthy Magistrates, to send forth a hundred well appointed soldiers, under the conduct of Captain John Hendicot, and in company with him that had command, Captain John Underbill, Captain Nathan Turner, Captain William Jenningson, besides other inferior officers. I would not have the world wonder at the great number of commanders to so few men, but know that the Indians' fight far differs from the Christian practice; for they most commonly divide themselves into small bodies, so that we are forced to neglect our usual way, and to subdivide our divisions to answer theirs, and not thinking it any disparagement to any captain to go forth against an enemy with a squadron of men, taking the ground from the old and ancient practice, when they chose captains of hundreds and captains of thousands, captains of fifties and captains of tens. We conceive a captain signifieth the chief in way of command of any body committed to his charge for the time being, whether of more or less, it makes no matter in power, though in honor it does. Coming to an anchor before the island, we espied an Indian walking by the shore in a desolate manner, as though he had received intelligence of our coming. Which Indian gave just ground to some to conclude that the body of the people had deserted the island.

But some knowing them for the generality to be a warlike nation, a people that spend most of their time in the study of warlike policy, were not persuaded that they would upon so slender terms forsake the island, but rather suspected they might lie behind a bank, much like the form of a barricado. Myself with others rode with a shallop, made towards the shore, having in the boat a dozen armed soldiers. Drawing near to the place of landing, the number that rose from behind the barricado were between fifty or sixty able fighting men, men as straight as arrows, very tall, and of active bodies, having their arrows notched. They drew near to the water side, and let fly at the soldiers, as though they had meant to have made an end of us all in a moment. They shot a young gentleman in the neck through a collar, for stiffness as if it had been an oaken board, and entered his flesh a good depth. Myself received an arrow through my coat sleeve, a second against my helmet on the forehead; so as if God in his providence had not moved the heart of my wife to persuade me to carry it along with me, (which I was unwilling to do), I had been slain. Give me leave to observe two things from hence; first, when the hour of death is not yet come, you see God useth weak means to keep his purpose unviolated; secondly, let no man despise advice and counsel of his wife, though she be a woman. It were strange to nature to think a man should be bound to fulfil the humor of a woman, what arms he should carry; but you see God will have it so, that a woman should overcome a man. What with Delilah's flattery, and with her mournful tears, they must and will have their desire, when the hand of God goes along in the matter; and this is to accomplish his own will. Therefore let the clamor bn quenched I daily hear in my ears, that New England men usurp over their wives, and keep them in servile subjection. The country is wronged in this matter, as in many things else. Let this precedent satisfy the doubtful, for that comes from the example of a rude soldier. If they be so courteous to their wives, as to take their advice in warlike matters, how much more kind is the tender, affectionate husband to honor his wife as the weaker vessel? Yet mistake not. I say not that they are bound to call their wives in council, though they are bound to take their private advice (so far as they see it make for their advantage and their good); instance Abraham. But to the matter. The arrows flying thick about us, we made haste to the shore; but the surf of the sea being great, hindered us, so as we could scarce discharge a musket, but were forced to make haste to land. Drawing near the shore through the strength of wind, and the hollow ness of the sea, we durst not adventure to run ashore, but were forced to wade up to the middle; but once having got up off our legs, we gave fire upon them. They finding our bullets to outreach their arrows, they fled before us. In the meanwhile Colonel Hindecot made to the shore, and some of this number also repulsed him at his landing, but hurt none. We thought they would stand it out with us, but they perceiving we were in earnest, fled; and left their wigwams, or houses, and provision to the use of our soldiers. Having set forth our sentinels, and laid out our pardues, we betook ourselves to the guard, expecting hourly they would fall upon us; but they observed the old rule, 'Tis good sleeping in a whole skin, and left us free from an alarm.

The next day we set upon our march, the Indians being retired into swamps, so as we could not find them. We burnt and spoiled both houses and corn in great abundance; but they kept themselves in obscurity. Captain Turner stepping aside to a swamp, met with some few Indians, and charged upon them, changing some few bullets for arrows. Himself received a shot upon the breast of his corselet, as if it had been pushed with a pike, and if he had not had it on, he had lost his life.

A pretty passage worthy observation. We had an Indian with us that was an interpreter; being in English clothes, and a gun in his hand, was spied by the islanders, which called out to him, What are you, an Indian or an Englishman? Come hither, saith he, and I will tell you. He pulls up his cock and let fly at one of them, and without question was the death of him. Having spent that day in burning and spoiling the island, we took up the quarter for that night. About midnight myself went out with ten men about two miles from our quarter, and discovered the most eminent plantation they had in the island, where was much corn, many wigwams, and great heaps of mats; but fearing less we should make an alarm by setting fire on them, we left them as we found them, and peaceably departed to our quarter; and the next morning with forty men marched up to the same plantation, burnt their houses, cut down their corn, destroyed some of their dogs instead of men, which they left in their wigwams.

Passing on toward the water side to embark our soldiers, we met with several famous wigwams, with great heaps of pleasant corn ready shelled; but not able to bring it away, we did throw their mats upon it, and set fire and burnt it. Many well-wrought mats our soldiers brought from thence, and several delightful baskets. We being divided into two parts, the rest of the body met with no less, I suppose, than ourselves did. The Indians playing least in sight, we spent our time, and could no more advantage ourselves than we had already done, and having slain some fourteen, and maimed others, we embarked ourselves, and set sail for Seasbrooke fort, where we lay through distress of weather four days; then we departed.

The Pequeats having slain one Captain Norton, and Captain Stone, with seven more of their company, order was given us to visit them, sailing along the Nahanticot shore with five vessels. The Indians spying of us came running in multitudes along the water side, crying, What cheer, Englishmen, what cheer, what do you come for? They not thinking we intended war, went on cheerfully until they come to Pequeat river. We thinking it the best way, did forbear to answer them; first, that we might the better be able to run through the work; secondly, that by delaying of them, we might drive them in security, to the end we might have the more advantage of them. But they seeing we would make no answer, kept on their course, and cried, What, Englishmen, what cheer, what cheer, are you hoggery, will you cram us? That is, are you angry, will you kill us, and do you come to fight? That night the Nahanticot Indians, and the Pequeats, made fire on both sides of the river, fearing we would land in the night. They made most doleful and woful cries all the night, (so that we could scarce rest) hallooing one to another, and giving the word from place to place, to gather their forces together, fearing the English were come to war against them.

The next morning they sent early aboard an ambassador, a grave senior, a man of good understanding, portly carriage, grave and majestical in his expressions. He demanded of us what the end of our coming was. To which we answered, that the governors of the Bay sent us to demand the heads of those persons that had slain Captain Norton and Captain Stone, and the rest of their company, and that it was not the custom of the English to suffer murderers to live; and therefore, if they desired their own peace and welfare, they will peaceably answer our expectation, and give us the heads of the murderers.

They being a witty and ingenious nation, their ambassador labored to excuse the matter, and answered, We know not that any of ours have slain any English. True it is, saith he, we have slain such a number of men; but consider the ground of it. Not long before the coming of these English into the river, there was a certain vessel that came to us in way of trade. We used them well, and traded with them, and took them to be such as would not wrong us in the least matter. But our sachem or prince coming aboard, they laid a plot how they might destroy him; which plot discovered itself by the event, as followeth. They keeping their boat aboard, and not desirous of our company, gave us leave to stand hallooing ashore, that they underhill's narrative. 57 might work their mischievous plot. But as we stood they called to us, and demanded of us a bushel of wampam-peke, which is their money. This they demanded for his ransom. This peal did ring terribly in our ears, to demand so much for the life of our prince, whom we thought was in the hands of honest men, and we had never wronged them. But we saw there was no remedy; their expectation must be granted, or else they would not send him ashore, which they promised they would do, if we would answer their desires. We sent them so much aboard, according to demand, and they, according to their promise, sent him ashore, [1] but first slew him. This much exasperated our spirits, and made us vow a revenge. Suddenly after came these captains with a vessel into the river, and pretended to trade with us, as the former did. We did not discountenance them for the present, but took our opportunity and came aboard. The sachem's son succeeding his father, was the man that came into the cabin of Captain Stone, and Captain Stone having drunk more than did him good, fell backwards on the bed asleep. The sagamore took his opportunity, and having a little hatchet under his garment, therewith knocked him in the head. Some being upon the deck and others under, suspected some such thing; for the rest of the Indians that were aboard had order to proceed against the rest at one time; but the English spying treachery, run immediately into the cook-room, and, with a fire-brand, had thought to have blown up the Indians by setting fire to the powder. These devil's instruments spying this plot of the English, leaped overboard as the powder was a firing, and saved themselves; but all the English were blown up. This was the manner of their bloody action. Saith the ambassador to us, Could ye blame us for revenging so cruel a murder? for we distinguish not between the Dutch and English, but took them to be one nation, and therefore we do not conceive that we wronged you, for they slew our king; and thinking these captains to be of the same nation and people as those that slew him, made us set upon this course of revenge.

Our answer was, They were able to distinguish between Dutch and English, having had sufficient experience of both nations; and therefore, seeing you have slain the king of England's subjects, we come to demand an account of their blood, for we ourselves are liable to account for them. The answer of the ambassador was, We know no difference between the Dutch and the English; they are both strangers to us, we took them to be all one; therefore we crave pardon; we have not wilfully wronged the English. — This excuse will not serve our turns, for we have sufficient testimony that you know the English from the Dutch. We must have the heads of those persons that have slain ours, or else we will fight with you. He answered, Understanding the ground of your coming, I will entreat you to give me liberty to go ashore, and I shall inform the body of the people what your intent and resolution is; and if you will stay aboard, I will bring you a sudden answer.

We did grant him liberty to get ashore, and ourselves followed suddenly after before the war was proclaimed. He seeing us land our forces, came with a message to entreat us to come no nearer, but stand in a valley, which had between us and them an ascent, that took our sight from them; but they might see us to hurt us, to our prejudice. Thus from the first beginning to the end of the action, they carried themselves very subtilely; but we, not willing to be at their direction, marched up to the ascent, having set our men in battalia. He came and told us he had inquired for the sachem, that we might come to a parley; but neither of both of the princes were at home; they were gone to Long Island.

Our reply was, We must not be put off thus, we know the sachem is in the plantation, and therefore bring him to us, that we may speak with him, or else we will beat up the drum, and march through the country, and spoil your corn. His answer, If you will but stay a little while, I will step to the plantation and seek for them. We gave them leave to take their own course, and used as much patience as ever men might, considering the gross abuse they offered us, holding us above an hour in vain hopes. They sent an Indian to tell us that Mommenoteck was found, and would appear before us suddenly. This brought us to a new stand the space of an hour more. There came a third Indian persuading us to have a little further patience, and he would not tarry, for he had assembled the body of the Pequeats together, to know who the parties were that had slain these Englishmen. But seeing that they did in this interim convey away their wives and children, and bury their chiefest goods, we perceived at length they would fly from us; but we were patient and bore with them, in expectation to have the greater blow upon them. The last messenger brought us this intelligence from the sachem, that if we would but lay down our arms, and approach about thirty paces from them, and meet the heathen prince, he would cause his men to do the like, and then we shall come to a parley.

But we seeing their drift was to get our arms, we rather chose to beat up the drum and bid them battle. Marching into a champaign field we displayed our colors; but none would come near us, but standing remotely off did laugh at us for our patience. We suddenly set upon our march, and gave fire to as many as we could come near, firing their wigwams, spoiling their corn, and many other necessaries that they had buried in the ground we raked up, which the soldiers had for booty. Thus we spent the day burning and spoiling the country. Towards night embarked ourselves. The next morning, landing on the Nahanticot shore, where we were served in like nature, no Indians would come near us, but run from us, as the deer from the dogs. But having burnt and spoiled what we could light on, we embarked our men, and set sail for the Bay. Having ended this exploit, came off, having one man wounded in the leg; but certain numbers of their slain, and many wounded. This was the substance of the first year's service. Now followeth the service performed in the second year.

This insolent nation, seeing we had used much lenity towards them, and themselves not able to make good use of our patience, set upon a course of greater insolence than before, and slew all they found in their way. They came near Seabrooke fort, and made many proud challenges, and dared them out to fight.

The lieutenant went out with ten armed men, and starting three Indians they changed some few shot for arrows. Pursuing them, a hundred more started out of the ambushments, and almost surrounded him and his company; and some they slew, others they maimed, and forced them to retreat to their fort, so that it was a special providence of God that they were not all slain. Some of their arms they got from them, others put on the English clothes, and came to the fort jeering of them, and calling, Come and fetch your Englishmen's clothes again; come out and fight, if you dare; you dare not fight; you are all one like women. We have one amongst us that if he could kill but one of you more, he would be equal with God, and as the Englishman's God is, so would he be. This blasphemous speech troubled the hearts of the soldiers, but they knew not how to remedy it, in respect of their weakness.

The Conetticot plantation, understanding the insolence of the enemy to be so great, sent down a certain number of soldiers, under the conduct of Captain John Mason, for to strengthen the fort. The enemy lying hovering about the fort, continually took notice of the supplies that were come, and forebore drawing near it as before; and letters were immediately sent to the Bay, to that right worshipful gentleman, Master Henry Vane, for a speedy supply to strengthen the fort. For assuredly without supply suddenly came, in reason all would be lost, and fall into the hands of the enemy. This was the trouble and perplexity that lay upon the spirits of the poor garrison. Upon serious consideration, the governor and council sent forth myself, with twenty armed soldiers, to supply the necessity of those distressed persons, and to take the government of that place for the space of three months. Relief being come, Captain John Mason, with the rest of his company, returned to the plantation again. We sometimes fell out, with a matter of twenty soldiers, to see whether we could discover the enemy or no. They seeing us (lying in ambush) gave us leave to pass by them, considering we were too hot for them to meddle with us. Our men being completely armed, with corselets, muskets, bandoleers, rests, and swords, (as they themselves related afterward), did much daunt them. Thus we spent a matter of six weeks before we could have anything to do with them, persuading ourselves that all things had been well. But they seeing there was no advantage more to be had against the fort, they enterprised a new action, and fell upon Watertowne, now called Wethersfield, with two hundred Indians. Before they came to attempt the place, they put into a certain river, an obscure small river running into the main, where they encamped, and refreshed themselves, and fitted themselves for their service, and by break of day attempted their enterprise, and slew nine men, women and children. Having finished their action, they suddenly returned again, bringing with them two maids captives, having put poles in their canoes, as we put masts in our boats, and upon them hung our English men's and women's shirts and smocks, instead of sails, and in way of bravado came along in sight of us as we stood upon Seybrooke fort. And seeing them pass along in such a triumphant manner, we much fearing they had enterprised some desperate action upon the English, we gave fire with a piece of ordnance, and shot among their canoes. And though they were a mile from us, yet the bullet grazed not above twenty yards over the canoe, where the poor maids were. It was a special providence of God it did not hit them, for then should we have been deprived of the sweet observation of God's providence in their deliverance. We were not able to make out after them, being destitute of means, boats, and the like. Before we proceed any farther to a full relation of the insolent proceeding of this barbarous nation, give me leave to touch upon the several accommodations that belong to this Seybrooke fort.

This fort lies upon a river called Conetticot, at the mouth of it, a place of a very good soil, good meadow, divers sorts of good wood, timber, variety of fish of several kinds, fowl in abundance, geese, ducks, brankes, teals, deer, roebuck, squirrels, which are as good as our English rabbits. Pity it is so famous a place should be so little regarded. It lies to the northwest of that famous place called Queenapiok, which rather exceeds the former in goodness. It hath a fair river, fit for harboring of ships, and abounds with rich and goodly meadows. This lies thirty miles from the upper plantations, which are planted on the river Conetticot. Twelve miles above this plantation is situated a place called Aguawam, no way inferior to the forenamed places. This country and those parts do generally yield a fertile soil, and good meadow all the rivers along. The river Conetticot is navigable for pinnaces miles; it hath a strong fresh stream that descends out of the hills. The tide flows not about half way up the river. The strength of the freshet that comes down the river is so strong, that it stoppeth the force of the tide.

The truth is, I want time to set forth the excellence of the whole country; but if you would know the garden of New England, then must you glance your eye upon Hudson's river, a place exceeding all yet named. The river affords fish in abundance, as sturgeon, salmon, and many delicate varieties of fish that naturally lies in the river; the only place for beaver that we have in those parts. Long Island is a place worth the naming, and generally affords most of the aforesaid accommodations. Nahanticot, Martin's Vineyard, Pequeat, Narragansett Bay, Elizabeth Islands, all these places are yet uninhabited, and generally afford good accommodation; as a good soil, according as we have expressed, they are a little inferior to the former places. The Narraganset Bay is a place for shipping, so spacious, as it will contain ten thousand sail of ships. Capcod, New Plimouth, Dukesbury, and all those parts, well accommodated for the receiving of people, and yet few are there planted, considering the spaciousness of the place. The Bay itself, although report goes it is full, and can hardly entertain any more, yet there are but few towns but are able to receive more than they have already, and to accommodate them in a comfortable measure.

The northern plantations, and eastern, as Puscataway, would not be neglected; they are desirable places, and lie in the heart of fishing. Puscataway is a river navigable for a ship of a hundred tons some six leagues up. With boats and pinnaces you may go a great way further. It is the only key of the country for safety. With twelve pieces of ordnance, will keep out all the enemies in the world. The mouth of the river is narrow, lies full upon the southeast sea; so as there is no anchoring without, except you hazard ship and men. It is accommodated with a good soil, abundance of good timber; meadows are not wanting to the place. Pity it is it hath been so long neglected.

Augumeaticus is a place of good accommodation; it lies five miles from Puscataway river, where Sir Ferdinando Gorge hath a house. It is a place worthy to be inhabited, a soil that bears good corn, all sorts of grain, flax, hemp, the country generally will afford. There was grown in Puscataway the last year, and in the Bay, as good English grain as can grow in any part of the world. Casko hath a famous bay, accommodated with a hundred islands, and is fit for plantation, and hath a river belonging to it, which doth afford fish in abundance, fowl also in great measure. So full of fowl it is, that strangers may be supplied with variety of fowl in an hour or two after their arrival, which knew not how to be relieved before. Because the place in general is so famous, and well known to all the world, and chiefly to our English nation (the most noblest of this Commonwealth), I therefore forbear many particulars which yet might be expressed.   And in regard of many aspersions hath been cast upon all the country, that it is a hard and difficult place for to subsist in, and that the soil is barren, and bears little that is good, and that it can hardly receive more people than those that are there, I will presume to make a second digression from the former matter, to the end I might encourage such as desire to plant there.

There are certain plantations, Dedham, Concord, in the Mathethusis Bay, that are newly erected, that do afford large accommodation, and will contain abundance of people. But I cease to spend time in matters of this nature, since my discourse tends to warlike story. But I crave pardon for my digression.

I told you before, that when the Pequeats heard and saw Seabrooke fort was supplied, they forbore to visit us. But the old serpent, according to his first malice, stirred them up against the church of Christ, and in such a furious manner, as our people were so far disturbed and affrighted with their boldness that they scarce durst rest in their beds; threatening persons and cattle to take them, as indeed they did. So insolent were these wicked imps grown, that like the devil, their commander, they run up and down as roaring lions, compassing all corners of the country for a prey, seeking whom they might devour. It being death to them for to rest without some wicked employment or other, they still plotted how they might wickedly attempt some bloody enterprise upon our poor native countrymen.

One Master Tilly, master of a vessel, being brought to an anchor in Conetticot river, went ashore, not suspecting the bloody-mindedness of those persons, who fell upon him and a man with him, whom they wickedly and barbarously slew; and, by relation, brought him home, tied him to a stake, flayed his skin off, put hot embers between the flesh and the skin, cut off his fingers and toes, and made hatbands of them; thus barbarous was their cruelty! Would not this have moved the hearts of men to hazard blood, and life, and all they had, to overcome such a wicked, insolent nation? But letters coming into the Bay, that this attempt was made upon Wethersfield in Conetticot river, and that they had slain nine men, women and children, and taken two maids captives, the council gave order to send supply. In the mean while the Conetticot plantations sent down one hundred armed soldiers, under the conduct of Captain John Mason, and Lieutenant Seily, with other inferior officers, who by commission were bound for to come to rendezvous at Seabrooke fort, and there to consult with those that had command there, to enterprise some stratagem upon these bloody Indians. The Conetticot company having with them threescore Mohiggeners, whom the Pequeats had drove out of their lawful possessions, these Indians were earnest to join with the English, or at least to be under their conduct, that they might revenge themselves of those bloody enemies of theirs. The English, perceiving their earnest desire that way, gave them liberty to follow the company, but not to join in confederation with them; the Indians promising to be faithful, and to do them what service lay in their power. But having embarked their men, and coming down the river, there arose great jealousy in the hearts of those that had chief oversight of the company, fearing that the Indians in time of greatest trial might revolt, and turn their backs against those they professed to be their friends, and join with the Pequeats. This perplexed the hearts of many very much, because they had had no experience of their fidelity. But Captain

Mason having sent down a shallop to Seybrooke fort, and sent the Indians over land to meet and rendezvous at Seabrooke fort, themselves came down in a great massy vessel, which was slow in coming, and very long detained by cross winds. The Indians coming to Seabrooke, were desirous to fall out on the Lord's day, to see whether they could find any Pequeats near the fort; persuading themselves that the place was not destitute of some of their enemies. But it being the Lord's day, order was given to the contrary, and wished them to forbear until the next day. Giving them liberty, they fell out early in the morning, and brought home five Pequeats' heads, one prisoner, and mortally wounded the seventh. This mightily encouraged the hearts of all, and we took this as a pledge of their further fidelity. Myself taking boat, rowed up to meet the rest of the forces. Lying aboard the vessel with my boat, the minister, one Master Stone, that was sent to instruct the company, was then in prayer solemnly before God, in the midst of the soldiers; and this passage worthy observation I set down, because the providence of God might be taken notice of, and his name glorified, that is so ready for to honor his own ordinance. The hearts of all in general being much perplexed, fearing the infidelity of these Indians, having not heard what an exploit they had wrought, it pleased God to put into the heart of Master Stone this passage in prayer, while myself lay under the vessel and heard it, himself not knowing that God had sent him a messenger to tell him his prayer was granted. O Lord God, if it be thy blessed will, vouchsafe so much favor to thy poor distressed servants, as to manifest one pledge of thy love, that may confirm us of the fidelity of these Indians towards us, that now pretend friendship and service to us, that our hearts may be encouraged the more in this work of thine. Immediately myself stepping up, told him that God had answered his desire, and that I had brought him this news, that those Indians had brought in five Pequeats' heads, one prisoner, and wounded one mortally; which did much encourage the hearts of all, and replenished them exceedingly, and gave them all occasion to rejoice and be thankful to God. A little before we set forth, came a certain ship from the Dutch plantation. Casting an anchor under the command of our ordnance, we desired the master to come ashore. The master and merchant, willing to answer our expectation, came forth, and sitting with us awhile unexpectedly revealed their intent, that they were bound for Pequeat river to trade. Ourselves knowing the custom of war, that it was not the practice, in a case of this nature, to suffer others to go and trade with them our enemies, with such commodities as might be prejudicial unto us, and advantageous to them, as kettles, or the like, which make them arrow-heads, we gave command to them not to stir, alleging that our forces were intended daily to fall upon them. This being unkindly taken, it bred some agitations between their several commanders; but God was pleased, out of his love, to carry things in such a sweet, moderate way, as all turned to his glory, and his people's good.

These men, seeing they could not have liberty to go upon their design, gave us a note under their hands, that if we would give them liberty to depart, they would endeavor, to the utmost of their ability, to release those two captive maids, and this should be the chief scope and drift of their design. Having these promises, depending upon their faithfulness, we gave them liberty. They set sail and went to Pequeat river, and sent to shore the master of the vessel to Sasacoose, their prince, for to crave liberty to trade; and what would they trade for but the English maids? which he much disliked. Suddenly withdrawing himself he returned back to the vessel, and by way of policy allured seven Indians into the bark, some of them being their prime men. Having them aboard, acquainted them with their intent, and told them without they might have the two captives delivered safely aboard, they must keep them as prisoners and pledges, and therefore must resolve not to go ashore, until such time they had treated with the sagamore. One of the Dutch called to them on the shore, and told them they must bring the two captive maids, if they would have the seven Indians; and therefore, briefly, if you will bring them, tell us; if not, we set sail, and will turn all your Indians overboard in the main ocean, so soon as ever we come out. They taking this to be a jest, slighted what was said unto them. They weighing anchor set sail, and drew near the mouth of the river. The Pequeats then discerned they were in earnest, and earnestly desired them to return and come to an anchor, and they would answer their expectation. So they brought the two maids, and delivered them safely aboard, and they returned to them the seven Indians. Then they set sail and came to Seabrooke fort. Bringing them to Seabrooke fort, request was made to have them ashore. But in regard of the Dutch governor's desire, who had heard that there was two English maids taken captives of the Pequeats, and thinking his own vessel to be there a trading with them, he had managed out a pinnace purposely, to give strict order and command to the former vessel to get these captives, what charge soever they were at, nay, though they did hazard their peace with them, and to gratify him with the first sight of them after their deliverance. So they earnestly entreated us that they might not be brought ashore so as to stay there, or to be sent home until they had followed the governor's order; which willingly was granted to them, though it were thirty leagues from us; yet were they safely returned again, and brought home to their friends. Now for the examination of the two maids after they arrived at Seabrooke fort. The eldest of them was about sixteen years of age. Demanding of her how they had used her, she told us that they did solicit her to uncleanness; but her heart being much broken, and afflicted under that bondage she was cast in, had brought to her consideration these thoughts — How shall I commit this great evil and sin against my God? Their heart were much taken up with the consideration of God's just displeasure to them, that had lived under so prudent means of grace as they did, and had been so ungrateful toward God, and slighted that means, so that God's hand was justly upon them for their remissness in all their ways. Thus was their hearts taken up with these thoughts. The Indians carried them from place to place, and showed them their forts and curious wigwams and houses, and encouraged them to be merry. But the poor souls, as Israel, could not frame themselves to any delight or mirth under so strange a king. They hanging their harps upon the willow trees, gave their minds to sorrow; hope was their chiefest food, and tears their constant drink. Behind the rocks, and under the trees, the eldest spent her breath in supplication to her God; and though the eldest was but young, yet must I confess the sweet affection to God for his great kindness and fatherly love she daily received from the Lord, which sweetened all her sorrows, and gave her constant hope that God would not nor could not forget her poor distressed soul and body; because, saith she, his loving kindness appeareth to me in an unspeakable manner. And though sometimes, saith she, I cried out, David-like, I shall one day perish by the hands of Saul, I shall one day die by the hands of these barbarous Indians; and specially if our people should come forth to war against them. Then is there no hope of deliverance. Then must I perish. Then will they cut me off in malice. But suddenly the poor soul was ready to quarrel with itself. Why should I distrust God? Do not I daily see the love of God unspeakably to my poor distressed soul? And he hath said he will never leave me nor forsake me. Therefore I will not fear what man can do unto me, knowing God to be above man, and man can do nothing without God's permission. These were the words that fell from her mouth when she was examined in Seabrooke fort. I having command of Seabrooke fort, she spake these things upon examination, in my hearing.

Christian reader, give me leave to appeal to the hearts of all true affectioned Christians, whether this be not the usual course of God's dealing to his poor captivated children, the prisoners of hope, to distil a great measure of sweet comfort and consolation into their souls in the time of trouble, so that the soul is more affected with the sense of God's fatherly love, than with the grief of its captivity. Sure I am, that sanctified afflictions, crosses, or any outward troubles appear so profitable, that God's dear saints are forced to cry out, Thy loving kindness is better than life, than all the lively pleasures and profits of the world. Better a prison sometimes and a Christ, than liberty without him. Better in a fiery furnace with the presence of Christ, than in a kingly palace without him. Better in the lion's den, in the midst of all the roaring lions and with Christ, than in a downy bed with wife and children without Christ. The speech of David is memorable, that sweet affectionate prince and soldier, "How sweet is thy word to my taste; yea, sweeter than the honey and the honey-comb." He spake it by experience. He had the sweet relish of God's comforting presence, and the daily communion he had with the Lord, in the midst of all his distresses, trials, and temptations that fell upon him. And so the Lord deals to this day. The greater the captivities be of his servants, the contentions amongst his churches, the clearer God's presence is amongst his, to pick and cull them out of the fire, and to manifest himself to their souls, and bear them up, as Peter above the water, that they sink not.

But now, my dear and respected friends and fellow soldiers in the Lord, are not you apt to say, If this be the fruit of afflictions, I would I had some of those, that I might enjoy these sweet breathings of Christ in my soul, as those that are in afflictions. But beware of those thoughts, or else experience will teach all to recall or to unwish those thoughts, for it is against the course of Scripture to wish for evil, that good might come of it. We cannot expect the presence of Christ in that which is contrary to him, (a man laying himself open to trouble), but we are rather to follow Christ' s example, "Father, not my will, but thy will be done, in earth as it is in heaven." And when thou art brought thus prostrate before the Lord like an obedient child, ready to suffer what he will impose on thee; then if he think good to try us, we may exclude no trial, no captivity, though burdensome or tedious to nature, for they will appear sweet and sanctified in the issue, if they be of the Lord's laying on; specially when the Lord is pleased to impose trouble on his in way of trial (as he said to Israel of old — I did it to prove you, and to see what was in your hearts), whether a soul would not do as the foolish young man in the Gospel, cling more closer to his honor, or profit, or ease, or peace, or liberty, than to the Lord Jesus Christ. And therefore the Lord is pleased to exercise his people with trouble and afflictions, that he might appear to them in mercy, and reveal more clearly his free grace unto their souls. Therefore consider, dear brethren, and err not, neither to the right hand nor to the left, and be not as Ephraim, like an untamed heifer, that would not stoop unto the yoke. But stoop to God's afflictions, if he please to impose them, and fear them not when they are from God. And know that Christ cannot be had without a cross. They are inseparable. You cannot have Christ in his ordinances, but you must have his cross. Did ever any Christian read, that in the purest churches that ever were, that Christians were freed from the cross? Was not the cross carried after Christ? And Andrew must follow Christ, but not without a cross. He must take it, and bear it, and that upon his shoulders; implying, it was not a light cross, but weighty. Oh, let not Christians show themselves to be so forgetful, as I fear many are, of the old way of Christ. Ease is come into the world, and men would have Christ and ease. But it will not be in this world. Is the servant better than the master? No, he is not, neither shall he be. But you may demand what is meant by this cross. We meet with many crosses in the world, losses at home and abroad, in church and commonwealth. What cross doth Christ mean? Was it a cross to be destitute of a house to put his head in? Or was it his cross, that he was not so deliciously fed as other men? Or to be so mean, wanting honor as others had? Or was it that his habit was not answerable to the course of the world, or to be destitute of silver and gold, as it is the lot of many of God's saints to this day? This was not the cross of Christ. You shall not hear him complain of his estate, that it is too mean, or his lodging too bad, or his garments too plain; these were not the troubles of Christ; these are companions to the cross. But the chief cross that Christ had, was that the word of his Father could not take place in the hearts of those to whom it was sent, and suffering for the truth of his Father, that was Christ' s cross. And that is the cross, too, that Christians must expect, and that in the purest churches. And, therefore, why do you stand and admire at New England, that there should be contentions there, and differences there, and that for the truth of Christ? Do you not remember that the cross followed the church? Hath it not been already said that Christ's cross followed him, and Andrew must carry it? And that Paul and Barnabas will contend together for the truth's sake? And doth not the Apostle say, Contend for the truth (though not in a violent way)? Doth not Christ say, I came not to bring peace, but a sword? And why should men wonder at us, seeing that troubles and contentions have followed the purest churches since the beginning of the world to this day? Wherefore should we not look back to the Scriptures, and deny our own reason, and let that be our guide and platform? And then shall we not so much admire, when we know it is the portion of God' s church to have troubles and contentions. And when we know also it is God that brings them, and that for good to his church. Hath not God ever brought light out of darkness, good out of evil? Did not the breath of God's spirit sweetly breathe in the souls of these poor captives which we now related? And do we not ever find, the greater the afflictions and troubles of God's people be, the more eminent is his grace in the souls of his servants? You that intend to go to New England, fear not a little trouble.

More men would go to sea, if they were sure to meet with no storms. But he is the most courageous soldier, that sees the battle pitched, the drums beat an alarm, and trumpets sound a charge, and yet is not afraid to join in the battle. Show not yourselves cowards, but proceed on in your intentions, and abuse not the lenity of our noble prince, and the sweet liberty he hath from time to time given to pass and repass according to our desired wills. Wherefore do ye stop? Are you afraid? May not the Lord do this to prove your hearts, to see whether you durst follow him in afflictions or not? What is become of faith? I will not fear that man can do unto me, saith David, no, nor what troubles can do, but will trust in the Lord, who is my God.

Let the ends and aims of a man be good, and he may proceed with courage. The bush may be in the fire, but so long as God appears to Moses out of the bush, there is no great danger. More good than hurt will come out of it. Christ knows how to honor himself, and to do his people good, though it be by contrary means, which reason will not fathom. Look but to faith, and that will make us see plainly, that though afflictions for the present are grievous, as doubtless it was with these two captive maids, yet sweet and comfortable is the issue with all God's saints, as it was with them. But to go on.

Having embarked our soldiers, we weighed anchor at Seabrooke fort, and set sail for the Narraganset Bay, deluding the Pequeats thereby, for they expected us to fall into the Pequeat river; but crossing their expectation, bred in them a security. We landed our men in the Narraganset Bay, and marched over land above two days' journey before we came to Pequeat. Quartering the last night's march within two miles of the place, we set forth about one of the clock in the morning, having sufficient intelligence that they knew nothing of our coming. Drawing near to the fort, yielded up ourselves to God, and entreated his assistance in so weighty an enterprise. We set on our march to surround the fort; [2] Captain John Mason, approaching to the west end, where it had an entrance to pass into it; myself marching to the south side, surrounding the fort; placing the Indians, for we had about three hundred of them, without side of our soldiers in a ring battalia, giving a volley of shot upon the fort. So remarkable it appeared to us, as we could not but admire at the providence of God in it, that soldiers so unexpert in the use of their arms, should give so complete a volley, as though the finger of God had touched both match and flint. Which volley being given at break of day, and themselves fast asleep for the most part, bred in them such a terror, that they brake forth into a most doleful cry; so as if God had not fitted the hearts of men for the service, it would have bred in them a commiseration towards them. But every man being bereaved of pity, fell upon the work without compassion, considering the blood they had shed of our native countrymen, and how barbarously they had dealt with them, and slain, first and last, about thirty persons. Having given fire, we approached near to the entrance, which they had stopped full with arms of trees, or brakes. Myself approaching to the entrance, found the work too heavy for me, to draw out all those which were strongly forced in. We gave order to one Master Hedge, and some other soldiers, to pull out those brakes. Having this done, and laid them between me and the entrance, and without order themselves, proceeded first on the south end of the fort. But remarkable it was to many of us. Men that run before they are sent, most commonly have an ill reward. Worthy reader, let me entreat you to have a more charitable opinion of me (though unworthy to be better thought of) than is reported in the other book. [3] You may remember there is a passage unjustly laid upon me, that when we should come to the entrance I should put forth this question, Shall we enter? Others should answer again, What came we hither for else? It is well known to many, it was never my practice, in time of my command, when we are in garrison, much to consult with a private soldier, or to ask his advice in point of war; much less in a matter of so great a moment as that was, which experience had often taught me was not a time to put forth such a question; and therefore pardon him that hath given the wrong information. Having our swords in our right hand, our carbines or muskets in our left hand, we approached the fort, Master Hedge being shot through both arms, and more wounded. Though it be not commendable for a man to make mention of anything that might tend to his own honor, yet because I would have the providence of God observed, and his name magnified, as well for myself as others, I dare not omit, but let the world know, that deliverance was given to us that command, as well as to private soldiers. Captain Mason and myself entering into the wigwams, he was shot, and received many arrows against his head-piece. God preserved him from many wounds. Myself received a shot in the left hip, through a sufficient buff coat, that if I had not been supplied with such a garment, the arrow would have pierced through me. Another I received between neck and shoulders, hanging in the linen of my head-piece. Others of our soldiers were shot, some through the shoulders, some in the face, some in the head, some in the legs, Captain Mason and myself losing each of us a man, and had near twenty wounded. Most courageously these Pequeats behaved themselves. But seeing the fort was too hot for us, we devised a way how we might save ourselves and prejudice them. Captain Mason entering into a wigwam, brought out a firebrand, after he had wounded many in the house. Then he set fire on the west side, where he entered; myself set fire on the south end with a train of powder. The fires of both meeting in the centre of the fort, blazed most terribly, and burnt all in the space of half an hour. Many courageous fellows were unwilling to come out, and fought most desperately through the palisadoes, so as they were scorched and burnt with the very flame, and were deprived of their arms — in regard the fire burnt their very bowstrings — and so perished valiantly. Mercy did they deserve for their valor, could we have had opportunity to have bestowed it. Many were burnt in the fort, both men, women, and children. Others forced out, and came in troops to the Indians, twenty and thirty at a time, which our soldiers received and entertained with the point of the sword. Down fell men, women, and children; those that scaped us, fell into the hands of the Indians that were in the rear of us. It is reported by themselves, that there were about four hundred souls in this fort, and not above five of them escaped out of our hands. Great and doleful was the bloody sight to the view of young soldiers that never had been in war, to see so many souls lie gasping on the ground, so thick, in some places, that you could hardly pass along. It may be demanded, Why should you be so furious? (as some have said). Should not Christians have more mercy and compassion? But I would refer you to David' s war. When a people is grown to such a height of blood, and sin against God and man, and all confederates in the action, there he hath no respect to persons, but harrows them, and saws them, and puts them to the sword, and the most terriblest death that may be. Sometimes the Scripture declareth women and children must perish with their parents. Sometimes the case alters; but we will not dispute it now. We had sufficient light from the word of God for our proceedings. Having ended this service, we drew our forces together to battalia. Being ordered, the Pequeats came upon us with their prime men, and let fly at us; myself fell on scarce with twelve or fourteen men to encounter with them; but they finding our bullets to outreach their arrows, forced themselves often to retreat. When we saw we could have no advantage against them in the open field, we requested our Indians for to entertain fight with them. Our end was that we might see the nature of the Indian war;

which they granted us, and fell out, the Pequeats, Narragansets, and Mohigeners changing a few arrows together after such a manner, as I dare boldly affirm, they might fight seven years and not kill seven men. They came not near one another, but shot remote, and not point-blank, as we often do with our bullets, but at rovers, and then they gaze up in the sky to see where the arrow falls, and not until it is fallen do they shoot again. This fight is more for pastime, than to conquer and subdue enemies. But spending a little time this way, we were forced to cast our eyes upon our poor maimed soldiers, many of them lying upon the ground, wanting food and such nourishable things as might refresh them in this faint state. But we were not supplied with any such things whereby we might relieve them, but only were constrained to look up to God, and to entreat him for mercy towards them. Most were thirsty, but could find no water. The provision we had for food was very little. Many distractions seized upon us at the present. A chirurgeon we wanted; our chirurgeon, not accustomed to war, durst not hazard himself where we ventured our lives, but, like a fresh water soldier, kept aboard, and by this means our poor maimed soldiers were brought to a great strait and faintness, some of them swounding away for want of speedy help; but yet God was pleased to preserve the lives of them, though not without great misery and pain to themselves for the present. Distractions multiplying, strength and courage began to fail with many. Our Indians, that had stood close to us hitherto, were fallen into consultation, and were resolved for to leave us in a land we knew not which way to get out. Suddenly after their resolution, fifty of the Narraganset Indians fell off from the rest, returning home. The Pequeats spying them, pursued after them. Then came the Narragansets to Captain Mason and myself, crying, Oh help us now, or our men will be all slain. We answered, How dare you crave aid of us, when you are leaving of us in this distressed condition, not knowing which way to march out of the country? But yet you shall see it is not the nature of Englishmen to deal like heathens, to requite evil for evil, but we will succor you. Myself falling on with thirty men, in the space of an hour rescued their men, and in our retreat to the body, slew and wounded above a hundred Pequeats, all fighting men, that charged us both in rear and flanks. Having overtaken the body we were resolved to march to a certain neck of land that lay by the sea-side, where we intended to quarter that night, because we knew not how to get our maimed men to Pequeat river. As yet we saw not our pinnaces sail along, but feared the Lord had crossed them, which also the master of the barque much feared. We gave them order to set sail on the Narraganset Bay, about midnight, as we were to fall upon the fort in the morning, so that they might meet us in Pequeat river in the afternoon; but the wind being cross, bred in them a great perplexity what would become of us, knowing that we were but slenderly provided, both with munition and provision. But they being in a distracted condition, lifted up their hearts to God for help. About twelve of the clock the wind turned about and became fair; it brought them along in sight of us, and about ten o'clock in the morning carried them into Pequeat river. Coming to an anchor at the place appointed, the wind turned as full against them as ever it could blow. How remarkable this providence of God was, I leave to a Christian eye to judge. Our Indians came to us, and much rejoiced at our victories, and greatly, admired the manner of Englishmen's fight, but cried Mach it, mach it; that is, It is naught, it is naught, because it is too furious, and slays too many men. Having received their desires, they freely promised, and gave up themselves to march along with us, wherever we would go. God having eased us from that oppression that lay upon us, thinking we should have been left in great misery for want of our vessels, we diverted our thoughts from going to that neck of land, and faced about, marching to the river where our vessels lay at anchor. One remarkable passage. The Pequeats playing upon our flanks, one Sergeant Davis, a pretty courageous soldier, spying something black upon the top of a rock, stepped forth from the body with a carbine of three feet long, and, at a venture, gave fire, supposing it to be an Indian's head, turning him over with his heels upward. The Indians observed this, and greatly admired that a man should shoot so directly. The Pequeats were much daunted at the shot, and forbore approaching so near upon us. Being come to the Pequeat river we met with Captain Patrick, who under his command had forty able soldiers, who was ready to begin a second attempt. But many of our men being maimed and much wearied, we forbore that night, and embarked ourselves, myself setting sail for Seabrooke fort. Captain Mason and Captain Patrick marching over land, burned and spoiled the country between the Pequeat and Conetticot river, where we received them. The Pequeats having received so terrible a blow, and being much affrighted with the destruction of so many, the next day fell into consultation. Assembling their most ablest men together, propounded these three things. First, whether they would set upon a sudden revenge upon the Narragansets, or attempt an enterprise upon the English, or fly. They were in great dispute one amongst another. Sasachus, their chief commander, was all for blood; the rest for flight, Alleging these arguments: We are a people bereaved of courage, our hearts are sadded with the death of so many of our dear friends; we see upon what advantage the English lie; what sudden and deadly blows they strike; what advantage they have of their pieces to us, which are not able to reach them with our arrows at distance. They are supplied with everything necessary; they are flote and heartened in their victory. To what end shall we stand it out with them? We are not able; therefore let us rather save some than lose all. This prevailed. Suddenly after, they spoiled all those goods they could not carry with them, broke up their tents and wigwams, and betook themselves to flight. Sasachus, flying towards Conetticot plantation, quartered by the river side; there he met with a shallop sent down to Seabrooke fort, which had in it three men; they let fly upon them, shot many arrows into them. Courageous were the English, and died in their hands, but with a great deal of valor. The forces which were prepared in the Bay were ready for to set forth. Myself being taken on but for three months, and the soldiers willing to return to the Bay, we embarked ourselves, and set to sail. In our journey we met with certain pinnaces, in them a hundred able and well appointed soldiers, under the conduct of one Captain Stoughton, and other inferior officers; and in company with them one Mr. John Wilson, who was sent to instruct the company. These falling into Pequeat river, met with many of the distressed Indians. Some they slew, others they took prisoners.

Finis

[1] This was no ways true of the English, but a devised excuse.
[2] This fort, or palisado, was well nigh an acre of ground, which was surrounded with trees and half trees, set into the ground three feet deep, and fastened close one to another, as you may see more clearly described in the figure of it before the book.
[3] The other book here referred to, containing the charge of which Underhill complains, is Vincent's Relation of the Pequot War.

Biographical Notice of Philip Vincent

[The following sketch of Philip Vincent was printed in Massachusetts Historical Society *Collections,* Fourth Series, vol. i.]

Very little, or perhaps nothing, is to be found in the printed literature of England concerning this person, so that it is not surprising nothing could be told respecting him, when this extremely rare tract of his was reprinted in the sixth volume of the third series of the Collections of the Massachusetts Historical Society.

Yet he has been to a certain extent his own biographer, that is, as far as to the year 1630, in which year he drew up an excellent genealogical account of the ancient family from which he was descended, including the leading facts in his own life so far, when, however, he was but in the earlier period of middle life. This tract has never been printed, but I have had an opportunity of perusing it in manuscript, among the historical collections of an eminent antiquary of the seventeenth century, Dr. Nathaniel Johnston, of Pontefract in Yorkshire.

He deduces himself from a John Vincent, a younger son of the Vincents of Great Smeaton, near Richmond, in Yorkshire. This John settled at Braithwell, a village near to the ancient castle of Coningsborough, a castle of the princes of the House of York. This was in the reign of Henry the Fifth, and the Vincents were then and afterwards much employed by the lords of Coningsborough. From John descended Richard Vincent, who in early life served in the English and Imperial armies, and was in Calais at the time when it was taken by the Duke of Guise. He returned to Yorkshire, his native country, where he was the father of another Richard Vincent, who was the father of Philip.

This Richard is said by his son to have been a student of Gray's Inn, but never practised the law. He married Elizabeth, daughter of Thomas Rokeby, of Hotham, a distinguished Yorkshire family, by whom he had three sons, Thomas, Philip, and William.

Philip says that his father, mother, and a sister of his father, all died within seven weeks of each other, in 1617, and were all buried in Coningsborough church. But they died within a shorter space, if the extracts which have been sent me from the Coningsborough Register may be relied upon: —

"1617 June 6, buried Elizabeth, wife of Richard Vincent, gent.
June 19, buried Richard Vincent of Firsbie.
June 26, buried Jane Vincent."

Richard and Jane Vincent left no written wills, but declared their intention by word of mouth, Richard on June 17th, and Jane on June 18th. They directed that their property should be divided equally among the three sons.

Philip, son of Richard Vincent of Firsby, or Frisby, for the name is written both ways, was baptized at Coningsborough on November 23, 1600. He himself tells us, that he was of Peter House in the University Vincent's naerative. 89 of Cambridge, and that he took the degree of Master of Arts in that University. At about five-and-twenty he married Frances, daughter of Sir Christopher Heydon of Baconsthorpe in Norfolk, a friend of Camden, and the most learned English writer in defense of judicial astrology, widow of Henry Draper of Bromley in Kent. He was ordained, and in 1625 was presented to the Rectory of Stoke d'Abernon in Surrey, by Sir Francis Vincent, who, though having the same surname, was of a different family. This living he resigned on the 17th of August, 1629, and on November 30, 1630, he lost his wife, who was buried in the church of St. Andrew, London. She had brought him three children, Francis and John, who both died in infancy, and Henry, who was born in Cursitor's Alley, London, on the 20th of December, 1629.

Here we lose the benefit of his own narrative; and the next notice I have seen of him is in the Book of the Grants of Sir William Segar, Garter King at Arms, during the period of his holding the office, which has lately been added to the library of the British Museum, where it is numbered 12,225 of the Additional Manuscripts.

Among these grants is one to "Philip Vincent, clerk, M. A., of Stoke d'Aberon in Surrey," then sailing to Guiana. It recites his birth at Frisby, and his descent, as shown above, describes the arms usually borne by the Vincents of Braithwell and Frisby, but authorizes him to bear the coat of Colbey, a family from whom the Vincents acquired Smeaton. This coat was a remarkable one, viz. "Or, a cross sarcelee in pale and formee in fess Gules."

There is no date of this grant; but we may safely collect from it, that soon after the death of his wife he commenced a life of wandering and enterprise, after the manner of two or three of his near relations, and that in the first instance he sailed for Guiana, a tempting region to English imagination ever since the appearance of Sir Walter Raleigh's ill-advised tract. It may be presumed that this may have been about the year 1632.

We then hear nothing of him, till we find that he was in New England in 1637, the time of the Pequot war. I know now that he states in so many words that he was there at the time; but it may be inferred with reasonable certainty that he was in close communication with the persons actually in the war, from the minute particularity of his narrative. It does not, however, appear from it that he himself was present in the war, a fact he would have distinctly set forth had it been really so. We may perceive in a passage or two of this tract, that he was not insensible to the value of his honorable descent and alliance; as, for example, at p. 40 of the Society's edition: "The meanest of the vulgar is not incapable of virtue, and consequently neither of honour. Some actions of Plebians have elsewhere been taken for great achievements."

The book, the title of which has been placed at the head of this article, contains proof that Vincent, the author, was a scholar, in the verses "Ad Lectorem," prefixed and signed "P. Vincentius."

If it be thought that there is not yet sufficient to identify the "P. Vincentius" who wrote on the Pequot war with the Philip Vincent who was about to sail to Guiana about 1632, I refer to the next publication of a "P. Vincent," which appeared in the same year, 1638, in which he published his relation of the Pequot war. The Imprimatur of his American tract is dated November 9, 1637, and is signed G. R. Weckherlin; the Imprimatur of this second tract is signed by the same person, and is dated November 12, 1637, three days after the former. The Address to the Reader is subscribed, "Thine, P. Vincent"; but in the title-page the author is distinctly pointed out as being in orders, "Composed by Dr. Vincent, Theol." This, I think, must remove all doubt of the author of the Pequot war being the Philip Vincent, once rector of Stoke d' Abernon, who sailed for the western hemisphere in or about 1 632. This book shows that he had travelled in Germany, without, however, showing the precise time; though probably not long before it was published; so that, supposing that he actually was in New England at the time of the Pequot war, he must have returned to Europe soon after the war was over. The title of this tract is,—

"The Lamentation of Germany. Wherein as in a glass we may behold the miserable condition, and read the woful effects of Sin. Composed by Dr. Vincent, Theol. an eye-witness thereof; and illustrated by pictures, the more to affect the Reader, &c. — London, printed by E. G. for John Rothwell, and are to be sold at the sign of the Sun in St. Paul's Church Yard." 1638. 12mo.

The only copy I ever saw of this tract is in the library of the British Museum. But in 1835 there was in the Catalogue of Mr. Thorpe, the bookseller in Bedford Street, a volume, in which this tract was bound up with three others, all printed in 1638, which have every appearance of having been the productions of the same author. As I never saw any of them, I merely give the titles as they appear in Mr. Thorpe's Catalogue: —

"Warnings of Germany by Wonderful Signs and Strange Prodigies, with a brief Relation of the miserable events which ensued. 1638."

"Invasions of Germany, with all the Civil and bloody wars therein. 1638." This is said to have numerous fine portraits.

"Lacrymae Germaniae; or the Tears of Germany, unfolding her woful distress. 1638."

More of his history I know not; or of what became of his son. But his elder brother, Thomas Vincent, became the ancestor of a respectable family of the name, seated at Barnborough Grange in the Deanery of Doncaster. Of this family there is an ample account in my History of that Deanery, Vol. I. p. 377. It became extinct, in 1730, by the death of a Philip Vincent.

Joseph Hunter.

A Trve Relation of the late Battell fought in New England

between the English and the
Pequet Salvages.

In which were slaine and taken prisoners
about 700 of the Salvages, and those which
escaped, had their heads cut off
by the Mohocks:

With the present state of things there.

LONDON,
Printed by *Thomas Harper,* for *Nathanael Butter,*
and *John Bellamie,* 1638.

Ad Lectorem

Authoris carmen de Victoria hac Nov'-Anglica, 1637.

D Veit in Americam varios gens Angla colonos:
*   Et bene convenient sidera, terra, solum.*
Ast ferns hoc prohibet, solis vagabundus in arvis,
*   Insolitoque aliquos, incola, Marte necat.*
Quod simul invitas crimen pervenit ad aures
*   Angligenum, irato murmure cuncta fremunt.*
Tunc Iaesi justa arma movent, hostemque sequuntur,
*   Struxerat hand vanis qui munimenta locis.*
Invadunt vallum, palis sudibusque munitum:
*   (Pax erit: hoc uno solvitur ira modo.)*
Vndique concidunt omnes, pars una crematur:
*   Post, caesi aut capti, coetera turba luit.*
Vtraque Iaetatur Pequetanis Anglia victis,
*   Et uovus, oeternum hic figimur, hospes ait.*
Virginia exultat, vicina Novonia gaudet,
*   Signaque securae certa quietis habent.*
Plaudite qui colitis Mavortia sacra nepotes,
*   Et serat incultos tutus arator agros.*
Quae novus orbis erat, spiranti numine (Lector)
*   Anglia nascetur, qua? novus orbis erit.*

P. Vincentius.

Nihil obstare videtur quo minus haec
Relatio typis mandetur.

Novemb. ix. M.DCxxxvij.
G. R. Weckherlin.

A true relation of the late battle fought in New-England, between the English and Salvages, with the present state of things there.

New England (a name now every day more famous) is so called, because the English were the first discoverers, and are now the planters thereof. It is the eastern coast of the north part of America, upon the southwest adjoining to Virginia, and part of that continent, large and capable of innumerable people. It is in the same height with the north of Spain and south part of France, and the temper not much unlike; as pleasant, as temperate, and as fertile as either, if managed by industrious hands.

This is the stage. Let us in a word see the actors. The year 1620, a company of English, part out of the Low Countries, and some out of London and other parts, were sent for Virginia. But being cut short by want of wind, and hardness of the winter, they landed themselves in this country, enduring, with great hope and patience, all the misery that desert could put upon them, and employed their wits to make their best use of that then snow-covered land for their necessities. After two years' experience of the nature of the soil, commodities, and natives, they returned such intelligence to their masters, that others took notice of their endeavors and the place. Then some western merchants collected a stock, and employed it that way. But they discouraged through losses and want of present gain, some Londoners and others (men of worth) undertook it, with more resolution, building upon the old foundation. Hence a second plantation, adjoined to the other, but supported with better pillars and greater means. All beginnings are ever difficult. The half, saith the proverb, is more than the whole. Some errors were committed, and many miseries were endured. No man is wise enough to shun all evils that may happen; but patience and painfulness overcame all. The success proved answerable even to ambitious expectations, notwithstanding the impediments inevitable to such undertakings.

There is scarce any part of the world but habitable, though more commodiously by human culture. This part (though in its naturals) nourished many natives, distinguished into divers petty nations and factions. It were needless curiosity to dispute their original, or how they came hither. Their outsides say they are men, their actions they say are reasonable. As the thing is, so it operateth. Their correspondency of disposition with us, argueth all to be of the same constitution, and the sons of Adam, and that we had the same matter, the same mould. Only art and grace have given us that perfection which yet they want, but may perhaps be as capable thereof as we. They are of person straight and tall, of limbs big and strong, seldom seen violent, or extreme in any passion. Naked they go, except a skin about their waist, and sometimes a mantle about their shoulders. Armed are with bows and arrows, clubs, javelins, &c. But as soil, air, diet, and custom, make ofttimes a memorable difference in men's natures, so it is among these nations, whose countries there are like so many shires here, of which every one hath their sagamore, or king, who, as occasion urgeth, commandeth them in war, and ruleth them in peace. Those where the English pitched, have showed themselves very loving and friendly, and done courtesies beyond expectation for these new-come inmates; so that much hath been written of their civility and peaceful conversation, until this year.

But nature, heaven's daughter, and the immediate character of that divine power, as by her light she hath taught us wisdom, for our own defence, so by her fire she hath made us fierce, injurious, revengeful, and ingenious in the device of means for the offence of those we take to be our enemies. This is seen in creatures void of reason, much more in mankind. We have in us a mixture of all the elements, and fire is predominant when the humors are exagitated. All motion causeth heat; all provocation moveth choler; and choler inflamed becometh a phrensy, a fury, especially in barbarous and cruel natures. These things are conspicuous in the inhabitants of New England; in whose southernmost part are the Pequets, or Pequants, a stately, warlike people, which have been terrible to their neighbors, and troublesome to the English.

In February last they killed some English at Seabrooke, a southerly plantation beyond Cape Cod, at the mouth of the river of Connectacutt. Since that the lieutenant of the fort there, with ten men armed, went out to fire the meadows, and to fit them for mowing. Arriving there, he started three Indians, which he pursued a little way, thinking to cut them off. But presently they perceived themselves encompassed with hundreds of them, who let fly their arrows furiously, and came desperately upon the muzzles of their muskets, though the English discharged upon them with all the speed they could. Three Englishmen were there slain, others wounded. The eight that remained made their way through the salvages with their swords, and so got under the command of the cannon of the fort, (otherwise they had been all slain or taken prisoners), one of the wounded falling down dead at the fort gate. The Indians thus fleshed and encouraged, besieged the fort as near as they durst approach. The besieged presently despatched a messenger to the Governor at the Bay, to acquaint him with these sad tidings, who with all speed lent unto their aid Captain Underbill, with twenty soldiers. Not long after these salvages went to Water Towne, now called Wether field, and there fell upon some that were sawing, and slew nine more, whereof one was a woman, the other a child, and took two young maids prisoners, killing some of their cattle, and driving some away. Man's nature insulteth in victory and prosperity, and by good success is animated even in the worst of wicked actions. These barbarians triumphed and proceeded, drawing into their confederacy other Indians, as the Nyantecets, and part of the Mohigens, of whom about fifty chose rather to join with the English, and sat down at New-Towne, at Connectacut (now called Hereford, as the other town that went from Dorchester thither is called Windsore). Fame increaseth by flying. The former sad news was augmented by the report of sixty men slain at Master Pinchen's plantation, &c. which proved false. The Narragansets, neighbors to the Peqnets, sent word to the English, that the Pequets had solicited them to join their forces with them. Hereupon the Council ordered that none should go to work, nor travel, no, not so much as to church, without arms. A corps of guard of fourteen or fifteen soldiers was appointed to watch every night, and sentinels were set in convenient places about the plantations, the drum beating when they went to the watch, and every man commanded to be in readiness upon an alarm, upon pain of five pound. A day of fast and prayers was also kept. Forty more were sent to strengthen the former twenty that went to the fort, and fifty under the command of Captain Mason, which being conjoined were about one hundred. Two hundred more were to be sent after them with all expedition.

The fifty Mohigins that joined with the English, scouting about, espied seven Pequets, killed five of them outright, wounded the sixth mortally, took the seventh prisoner, and brought him to the fort. He braved the English, as though they durst not kill a Pequet. Some will have their courage to be thought invincible, when all is desperate. But it availed this salvage nothing. They tied one of his legs to a post, and twenty men, with a rope tied to the other, pulled him in pieces. Captain Underbill shooting a pistol through him, to despatch him. The two maids which were taken prisoners were redeemed by the Dutch.

Those fifty sent from the three plantations of Connectacut with Captain Mason, being joined with Captain Underhill and his twenty men, (for the other forty were not yet arrived with them), immediately went upon an expedition against the Pequets, after they had searched for them. The manner was this. The English with some Mohigens went to the Naragansets, who were discontented that they came no sooner, saying they could arm and set forth two or three hundred at six hours warning, (which they did accordingly, for the assistance of the English); only they desired the advice of the sagamore, Mydutonno, what way they should go to work, and how they should fall on the Pequets; whose judgment in all things agreed with the English, as though they had consulted together. Then went they to the Nyanticke, and he set forth two hundred more; but before they went, he swore them after his manner upon their knees. As they marched, they deliberated which fort of the Pequets they should assault, resolving upon the great fort, and to be there that night. Being on the way, and having a mile to march through swamps, the Nyanticke hearts failed, for fear of the Pequets, and so they ran away, as also did some of the Narragansets. Of five or six hundred Indians, not above half were left; and they had followed the rest, had not Captain Underhill upbraided them with cowardice, and promised them they should not fight or come within shot of the fort, but only surround it afar off. At break of day, the seventy English gave the fort a volley of shot, whereat the salvages within made a hideous and pitiful cry; the shot, without all question, flying through the palisadoes (which stood not very close) and killing or wounding some of them. Pity had hindered further hostile proceedings, had not the remembrance of the bloodshed, the captive maids, and cruel insolency of those Pequets, hardened the hearts of the English, and stopped their ears unto their cries. Mercy mars all sometimes; severe justice must now and then take place.

The long forbearance and too much lenity of the English towards the Virginian salvages, had like to have been the destruction of the whole plantation. These barbarians, ever treacherous, abuse the goodness of those that condescend to their rudeness and imperfections. The English went resolutely up to the door of the fort. What! shall we enter? said Captain Underhill. [1] What come we for else? answered one Hedge, a young Northamptonshire gentleman; who, advancing before the rest, plucked away some bushes, and entered. A stout Pequet encounters him, shoots his arrow, drawn to the head, into his right arm, where it stuck. He slashed the salvage betwixt the arm and shoulder, who, pressing towards the door, was killed by the English. Immediately Master Hedge encountered another, who perceiving him upon him before he could deliver his arrow, gave back; but he struck up his heels and run him through; after him he killed two or three more. Then about half the English entered, fell on with courage, and slew many. But being straitened for room because of the wigwams, (which are the salvage huts or cabins), they called for fire to burn them. An Englishman stepped into a wigwam, and stooping for a firebrand, an Indian was ready to knock out his brains: but he whipt out his sword and run him into the belly, that his bowels followed. Then were the wigwams set on fire, which so raged, that what therewith, what with the sword, in little more than an hour betwixt three and four hundred of them were killed, and of the English only two — one of them by our own muskets, as is thought. For the Naragansets beset the fort so close, that not one escaped. The whole work ended, ere the sun was an hour high, the conquerors retreated down toward the pinnace, but in their march were infested by the rest of the Pequets, who scouting up and down, from the swamps and thickets let fly their arrows a-main, which were answered by English bullets. The Indians that then assisted the English, waiting the fall of the Pequets, (as the dog watcheth the shot of the fowler, to fetch the prey), still fetched them their heads, as any were slain. At last the Narragansets perceiving powder and shot to fail, and fearing to fall into the hands of their enemies, betook themselves to flight upon the sudden, and were as suddenly encompassed by the Pequets. Fear defeateth great armies. If an apprehension of imminent danger once possess them, it is in vain to stay the runaways. No oratory can recall them, no command can order them again. The only sure way is, by all means that may be, promises, threats, persuasions, &c, to maintain and keep up courage, where yet it is. But these fearful companions had one anchor, whose cable was not broken. They sent speedily to the English, who came to their rescue; and after five muskets discharged, the Pequets fled. Thus freed from that fear, they vowed henceforth to cleave closer to the English, and never to forsake them in time of need. The reason why the English wanted ammunition was, because they had left that which they had for store, with their drum, at the place of their consultation; but found it in their return. They now all went ashipboard, and sailed to Seabrook fort, where the English feasted the Narragansets three days, and then sent them home in a pinnace.

Let me now describe this military fortress, which natural reason and experience hath taught them to erect, without mathematical skill, or use of iron tool. They choose a piece of ground, dry and of best advantage, forty or fifty foot square (but this was at least two acres of ground.) Here they pitch, close together as they can, young trees and half trees, as thick as a man's thigh or the calf of his leg. Ten or twelve foot high they are above the ground, and within rammed three foot deep with undermining, the earth being cast up for their better shelter against the enemy's dischargements. Betwixt these palisadoes are divers loopholes, through which they let fly their winged messengers. The door for the most part is entered sideways, which they stop with boughs or bushes, as need requireth. The space therein is full of wigwams, wherein their wives and children live with them. These huts or little houses are framed like our garden arbors, something more round, very strong and handsome, covered with close-wrought mats, made by their women, of flags, rushes, and hempen threads, so defensive that neither rain, though never so bad and long, nor yet the wind, though never so strong, can enter. The top through a square hole giveth passage to the smoke, which in rainy weather is covered with a pluver. This fort was so crowded with these numerous dwellings, that the English wanted foot-room to grapple with their adversaries, and therefore set fire on all.

The Mohigens which sided with the English in this action, behaved themselves stoutly; which the other Pequets understanding, cut off all the Mohigens that remain with them (lest they should turn to the English) except seven; who flying to our countrymen, related this news, and that about an hundred Pequets were slain, or hurt in the fight with the English, at their return from the fort; moreover, that they had resolved to have sent an hundred choice men out of their fort, as a party against the English, the very day after they were beaten out by them; but being now vanquished, Sasacus, the Pequetan captain, with the remainder of this massacre, was fled the country.

It is not good to give breath to a beaten enemy, lest he return armed, if not with greater puissance, yet with greater despite and revenge. Too much security, or neglect in this kind, hath ofttimes ruined the conquerors. The two hundred English, therefore, resolved on before, were now sent forth to chase the barbarians, and utterly root them out. Whereupon, Captain Underbill with his twenty men returned, and gave this account of those exploits of the

New Englanders, which here we have communicated to the old English world. This last party invaded the Pequetan country, killed twenty-three, saved the lives of two sagamores for their use hereafter, as occasion shall serve, who have promised to do great matters for the advancing of the English affairs. They pursued the remnant threescore miles beyond the country, till within six and thirty miles of the Dutch plantations on Hudson's river, where they fought with them, killed forty or fifty, besides those that they cut off in their retreat, and took prisoners one hundred and eighty, that came out of a swamp, and yielded themselves upon promise of good quarter. Some other small parties of them were since destroyed; and Captain Patrick, with sixteen or eighteen, brought eighty captives to the Bay of Boston. The news of the flight of Sassacus, their sagamore, is also confirmed. He went with forty men to the Mohocks, which are cruel, bloody cannibals, and the most terrible to their neighbors of all these nations; but will scarce dare ever to carry arms against the English, of whom they are sore afraid, not daring to encounter white men with their hot-mouthed weapons, which spit nothing else but bullets and fire.

The terror of victory changeth even the affection of the allies of the vanquished, and the securing of our own estates makes us neglect, yea forsake or turn against our confederates, and side with their enemies and ours, when we despair of better remedy. These cruel, but wily Mohocks, in contemplation of the English, and to procure their friendship, entertain the fugitive Pequets and their captain by cutting off all their heads and hands, which they sent to the English, as a testimony of their love and service.

A day of thanksgiving was solemnly celebrated for this happy success; the Pequetans now seeming nothing but a name, for not less than seven hundred are slain or taken prisoners. Of the English are not slain in all above sixteen. One occurrent I may not forget. The endeavors of private men are ever memorable in these beginnings; the meanest of the vulgar is not incapable of virtue, and consequently, neither of honor. Some actions of plebeians have elsewhere been taken for great achievements. A pretty sturdy youth of New Ipswich, going forth somewhat rashly to pursue the salvages, shot off his musket after them till all his powder and shot were spent; which they perceiving, re -assaulted him, thinking with their hatchets to have knocked him in the head: but he so bestirred himself with the stock of his piece, and after with the barrel, when that was broken, that he brought two of their heads to the army. His own desert, and the encouragement of others, will not suffer him to be nameless. He is called Francis Wainwright, and came over servant with one Alexander Knight, that kept an inn in Chelmsford.

I have done with this tragic scene, whose catastrophe ended in a triumph. And now give me leave to speak something of the present state of things there. The transcribing of all colonies is chargeable, fittest for princes or states to undertake. Their first beginnings are full of casualty and danger, and obnoxious to many miseries. They must be well grounded, well followed, and managed with great stocks of money, by men of resolution, that will not be daunted by ordinary accidents. The Bermudas and Virginia are come to perfection, from mean, or rather base beginnings, and almost by as weak means, beyond all expectation and reason. But a few private men, by uniting their stocks and desires, have now raised New England to that height, that never any plantation of Spaniards, Dutch, or any other arrived at, in so small a time. Gain is the loadstone of adventures; fish and furs, with beaver wool, were specious baits. But whilst men are all for their private profit, the public good is neglected, and languisheth. Woful experience had too evidently instructed New England's colonies in the precedents of Guiana, the Charibe islands, Virginia, and Novania or New-found-land, (now again to be planted by Sir David Kirke, though part of the old planters there yet remain). We are never wiser, than when we are thus taught. The New-Englanders, therefore, advanced the weal public all they could, and so the private is taken care for.

Corn and cattle are wonderfully increased with them, and thereof they have enough, yea sometime to spare to new comers, besides spare rooms or good houses to entertain them in; where they may make Christmas fires all winter, if they please, for nothing. I speak not of the naturals of the country, fish, fowl, &c, which are more than plentiful. They that arrived there this year out of divers parts of Old England, say, that they never saw such a field of four hundred acres of all sorts of English grain, as they saw at Winter-towne there. Yet that ground is not comparable to other parts of New England, as Salem, Ipswich, Newberry, &c. In a word, they have built fair towns of the land's own materials, and fair ships too, some whereof are here to be seen on the Thames; they have overcome cold and hunger, are dispersed securely in their plantations sixty miles along the coast, and within the land also, along some small creeks and rivers, and are assured of their peace, by killing the barbarians, better than our English Virginians were by being killed by them. For having once terrified them, by severe execution of just revenge, they shall never hear of more harm from them, except, perhaps, the killing of a man or two at his work, upon advantage, which their sentinels and corps-du-guards may easily prevent. Nay, they shall have those brutes their servants, their slaves, either willingly or of necessity, and docible enough, if not obsequious. The numbers of the English amount to above thirty thousand, which, (though none did augment them out of England), shall every day be, doubtless, increased, by a faculty that God hath given the British islanders, to beget and bring forth more children than any other nation of the world. I could justify what I say from the mouths of the Hollanders, and adjoining provinces, where they confess, (though good breeders of themselves), that never woman bore two children, nor yet had so many by one man, till the English and Scots frequented their wars, and married with them. I could give a good reason hereof from nature, as a philosopher, (with modesty be it spoken), but there is no need. The air of New England, and the diet, equal, if not excelling that of Old England: besides, their honor of marriage, and careful preventing and punishing of furtive congression, giveth them and us no small hope of their future puissance and multitude of subjects. Herein, saith the wise man, consisteth the strength of a king, and likewise of a nation, or kingdom.

But the desire of more gain, the slavery of mankind, was not the only cause of our English endeavors for a plantation there. The propagation of religion was Vincent's narrative. Ill that precious jewel for which these merchant ventures compassed both sea and land, and went into a far country to search and seat themselves. This I am sure they pretended, and I hope intended. Only this blessing from my heart I sincerely wish them, and shall ever beseech the Almighty to bestow upon them, devout piety towards God, faithful loyalty towards their sovereign, fervent charity among themselves, and discretion and sobriety in themselves, according to the saying of that blessed Apostle, Rom. xii. 3. Not to be wise (in spiritual things) above what w be wise unto wise sobriety.

Doubtless there was no
chastise the insolency of th
cides, than a sharp war pursu
and speed. Virginia our mother
for her precedent a rule, hath taught
do in these difficulties, forewarn
They were endangered by their
peace, secured by their enmity and
the natives. From these experimen
now inhabitants of those two sister
out unto themselves an armor
of lay a sure foundation to their future

Finis.

[1] Underhill denies this statement.

[Captain Lion Gardener's account of the war (as will be seen from his letter of June 12, 1660, printed herewith,) was drawn up partly from old papers and partly from memory. It remained in manuscript until 1833, when it was printed in 3. *Mass. Hist. Coll.,* III, 131-160. It is reprinted also in Penhallow's *Indian Wars* (edited by Dodge, Cincinnati, 1859,) as an appendix. It is, after Mason's, perhaps the best account. Gardener was a man of ability, a good soldier, and an actual participant in the leading events of the war. In the present reprint, Gardener's own spelling of his name is used in preference to that of a later date. — **Editor's Note.**]

Gardener's Narrative

Instructions from the Massachusetts to John Winthrop Esqr first Governour of Connecticut to Treat with The Pequots.

[The following manuscript Letter and Commission directed to John Winthrop Jun. Esq. , the first Governor of Connecticut, and signed by Sir Henry Vane, the Governor, and John Winthrop Esq. the Deputy Governor of Massachusetts, were found among the papers of the elder Gov. Trumbull of Connecticut in the year 1809, and were kindly furnished to the Publishing Committee of the Massachusetts Historical Society for publication in its Collections, by William T. Williams, Esq. of Lebanon, Con. The Society is also deeply indebted to Mr. Williams for several other manuscripts of interest published in this collection. These papers, it is understood, formerly belonged to the Connecticut branch of the Winthrop family. — *Publishing Committee, Mass. Hist. Soc*]

"Whereas it so falls out by the good Prouidence of God, that the place of your present residence is neare adjoyning unto certaine of the Natiues who are called the Pequots, concerning whom we haue diuers things to enquire and satisfy ourselues in; our request to you therefore is, and by these presents we do giue you full power, authority, and commission to treate and conferre with the sayd Pequots, in our names according to the instructions to these annexed, as if wee ourselues were present: and to make report backe agayne unto vs of the issue and successe of the whole before the next Generall Court (which, God willing is intended in the beginning of the 7th month). Thus recommending you, and your affayres to the blessing of Allmighty God, wee rest

Your louing freinds
HVane. Gov'
Jo: Winthrop Dep'
Massatuchets the 4th day
Of the 5th month. 1636."

"Massatuchets Month: 5ᵗʰ. 4. 1636.   The instructions which are recommended to John Winthrop Jun r Esq r in his negotiation with the Pequots.

"1. To giue notice to the principall Sachem that you haue receaued a commission from vs to demaund a solemne meeting for conference with them in a friendly manner about matters of importance.

"2. In case they slight such a message and refuse to giue you a meeting (at such place as yourself shall apoynt) then you are in our names to returne backe their present, (which you shall receaue from vs) and to acquaint them with all, that we hold ourselues free from any peace or league witn them as a people guilty of English blood.

"3. If they consent, and giue you a meeting as afore sayd, that then you lay downe vnto them how unworthily they haue requited our friendship with them; for as much as that they haue broken the very condition of the peace betwixt vs, by the not rendring into our hands the murtherers of Capt Stone, (which we desire you once agayne solemly to require of them), as also in that they so trifled with vs in their present which they made proffer of to vs, as that they did send but part of it, and put it off with this, as to say the old men did neuer consent to the giuing of it; which dealings sauour so much of dishonour and neglect, as that no people that desire friendship should put them in practice.

"4. To let them know first what credible relation hath beene given vs, that some of the cheif of them were actors in the murder of Mr Hamond and the other vpon Long Hand; and since of another Englishman there: and of their late determination to haue seized vpon a Plimouth Barke lying in their harbour for trade; as by the more large descriptions of these things, which we also send vnto you, will more distinctly appear. Of all these things we desire you to take the relation from their owne mouths, and to informe vs particularly of their seuerall answers: giuing them to vnderstand that it is not the manner of the English to take reuenge of injury vntill the partys that are guilty haue beene called to answer fairely for themselves.

"5. To let them know that if they shall cleare themselues of these matters, we shall not refuse to hearken to any reasonable proposition from them for confirmation of the peace betwixt vs. But if they shall not giue you satisfaction according to these our instructions, or shall bee found guilty of any of the sayd murthers, and will not deliuuer the actours in them into our hands, that then (as before you are directed) you returne them the present, and declare to them that we hold ourselues free from any league or peace with them, and shall reuenge the blood of our countrimen as occasion shall serue.

H: Vane Gov'
Jo: Winthrop Dep°'

Leift Lion Gardener his relation of the Pequot Warres

[The original manuscript of this "Relation" and a copy in the handwriting of Gov. Trumbull were furnished to the Publishing Committee by William T. Williams, Esq. The Committee, on account of the difficulty the printer would find in deciphering the original, have followed the orthography of the copy, excepting in the proper names, where they thought it of more importance to adhere to the ancient orthography. Mr. Williams in his interesting letters of July 19 and 23, 1832, addressed to a member of the Committee, has given some few particulars in relation to Lion Gardener; also a description of the battle-ground where the Pequots were destroyed, and of the burial place of Uncas and Miantunnomoh, together with a succinct account of the present condition of the remnant of the ancient and powerful tribes of the Pequots, Mohegans and Narragan sets. These portions of the letters are of historical value, and the Committee therefore take the liberty of publishing the following extracts. — *Publishing Committee, Mass. Hist. Soc.*]

"Lion Gardener was sent over by Lords Say and Seal and Lord Brook to construct a fort at the mouth of Connecticut river, to command it, &c. He was said to be a skilful engineer, and on that account was selected. He had seen some service in the Low Countries under Gen. Fairfax. He came into this Country about the year 1633 or 1634 [1] and erected the fort at Saybrook in Connecticut, which was so named in honour of Lords Say and Seal and Lord Brook: but how long he continued to command the fort I do not recollect. [2] He commanded it when Capt. John Mason conquered the Pequots, for Mason in his history, you recollect, says, ' he, Lt. Gardiner, complimented or entertained him with many big guns,' on his arrival at the fort after the conquest of the Pequots.

****

"Gardener continued some time in the command of the fort, but it does not appear when he left it. While he commanded it, he once very narrowly escaped being captured by the Pequots. He had five men with him, one of whom was taken and tortured; the fort was burnt down, and he and his family narrowly escaped being burnt in it. Gardener's Island, lying in Gardener's Bay, to which he removed and where he died, was taken possession of by him soon after his coming into this country. You will perceive he has reference to his island: it is a very beautiful island of good land, perhaps twenty - five hundred or three thousand acres, with a long sand point of not much value. It now wholly belongs to the family and was until the decease of the last proprietor, Jonathan Gardiner, an entailed estate; but I am told that the entail is now broken. The proprietors have always been called Lords.

****

"In the mouth of Mistic river there is an island, now and always called Mason's Island from old Capt. Mason, containing five or six hundred acres. This island he took possession of by right of conquest, and the most of it is now possessed by his descendants. I believe it is the only spot in Connecticut claimed in that way.

****

"Summer before last I went to the battle-ground on purpose to view it. The spot where the fort stood is in the present town of Groton, Connecticut, on the west side of Mistic river. Sassacus had this fort in the eastern part of his dominions to look after the Narragansetts. The hill is commanding and beautiful though not steep. The land is now owned by Roswell Fish, Esq. of Groton. There are no remains of the fort; Capt. Mason says it was of timber mostly, and of course when he burnt it, it must have been principally consumed. Mr. Fish told me that within his recollection (and he is about sixty) some few Indian arrowheads and spears have been found on the ground, and also some bullets. The river is at the bottom of the hill, less than half a mile, I should think, from the site of the fort, and perhaps three miles from the head of the little village of Mistic in the town of Stoning ton, where the small streams that form the river meet the tide water. The river is the dividing line between the towns of Groton and Stonington. Porter's rocks, where Capt. Mason lodged, are near the village, and perhaps two miles above the site of the fort.

"Sassacus had another fort, about two miles west of the one taken by Mason, in the town of Groton, from which the one taken was recruited on the night before the attack. The whole of the shore of Mistic river, which is about six or seven miles from what is called head of Mistic, to its mouth, and particularly the west side, is rough, rugged, and rocky, but particularly pleasant, and filled with dwellings wherever they can be placed, inhabited chiefly by sailors and seamen. There is a pretty meeting-house among the rocks.

******

"There is a remnant of the Pequots still existing. They live in the town of Groton, and amount to about forty souls, in all, or perhaps a few more or less; but do not vary much from that amount. They have about eleven acres of poor land reserved to them in Groton, on which they live. They are more mixed than the Mohegans with negro and white blood, yet are a distinct tribe and still retain a hatred to the Mohegans. A short time since, I had an opportunity of seeing most of the tribe together. They are more vicious, and not so decent or so good looking a people as the Mohegans. This however may be owing to their being more mixed with other blood. It is very rare that there are any intermarriages with either of the tribes to each other, they still, so far as circumstances admit, retaining the old grudge. The most common name among them is Meazen; nearly half call themselves by that surname.

"The Indians formerly called Ninegrate's men, seem to be now called the Narragansetts, and live principally in Charlestown, Rhode Island. There are perhaps eighty, or more; though I am not so well informed concerning them, as of the Pequots or Mohegans.

"Considerable exertion is making now in favor of the Mohegans. A small, but neat church, has lately been erected by charity for them, and the United States have appropriated nine hundred dollars to build a school-master's house, and for his salary. The house for the school-master is erected and a schoolmaster hired, who also preaches to the tribe. All of the tribe are anxiously sought out, and the benevolent are trying to bring them all together to their ancient seat. There are about seventy men on their land, or perhaps a few more. They own about three thousand acres of good land in Montville, about three miles below Norwich landing. The Trading Cove brook is their northern bound; their eastern is the Thames river. The General Assembly of this State, immediately after the Pequot war was finished, declared, and I think unfortunately, that the name of the Pequots should become extinct; that the river that used to be called Pequot should be called Thames; and the place called Pequot should no longer be so called, but its name be changed to New London, in "remembrance," as the records declare, and as the Assembly say, ' ' of the chief city in our dear native country."

"I have visited the ground where the rival chiefs, Uncas and Miantunnomoh, are buried. Uncas is buried in the royal burying ground, so called, which was appropriated to the Uncas family. It is just by the falls in the Yantic river in Norwich city; a beautiful and romantic spot. Calvin Goddard, Esq. of Norwich, owns the ground, and has (honorably) railed it in, and keeps it appropriated to its use. I saw him a few days since; he intends to enlarge it, and I hope to have an appropriate stone to mark the place. Miantunnomoh is buried in the east part of Norwich, at a place called Sachem's Plain, from the event of his death; and is buried on the spot where he was slain. But a few years since a large heap of stones, thrown together by the wandering Indians, according to the custom of their country, and as a melancholy mark of the love the Narragansets had for their fallen chief, lay on his grave: but the despicable cupidity of some people in that vicinity has removed them to make common stone wall, as it saved them the trouble of gathering stones for that purpose. The spot of his sepulture is, however, yet known."

East Hampton, June 12, 1660.

"Loving Friends, Robert Chapman and Thomas Hurlburt, my love remembered to you both, these are to inform, that as you desired me when I was with you and Major Mason at Seabrooke two years and an half ago to consider and to call to mind the passages of God's Providence at Seabrooke in and about the time of the Pequit [Pequot] War, wherein I have now endeavoured to answer your Desires and having rumaged and found some old papers then written it was a great help to my memory. You know that when I came to you I was an engineer or architect, whereof carpentry is a little part, but you know I could never use all the tools, for although for my necessity, I was forced sometimes to use my shifting chissel and my holdfast, yet you know I could never endure nor abide the smoothing plane; I have sent you a piece of timber scored and forehewed unfit to join to any handsome piece of work, but seeing I have done the hardest work, you must get somebody to chip it and to smooth it lest the splinters should prick some men's fingers, for the truth must not be spoken at all times, though to my knowledge I have written nothing but truth, and you may take out or put in what you please, or if you will, may throw it all into the fire; but I think you may let the Governor and Major Mason see it. I have also inserted some additions of things that were done since, that they may be considered together. And thus as I was when I was with you, so I remain still

Your loving friend,
Lion Gardener.

"In the year 1635, I, Lion Gardener, Engineer and Master of works of Fortification in the legers of the Prince of Orange, in the Low Countries, through the persuasion of Mr. John Davenport, Mr. Hugh Peters with some other well-affected Englishmen of Rotterdam, I made an agreement with the forenamed Mr. Peters for £100 per annum, for four years, to serve the company of patentees, namely, the Lord Say, the Lord Brooks [Brook,] Sir Arthur Hazilrig, Sir Mathew Bonnington [Bonighton?], Sir Richard Saltingstone [Saltonstall], Esquire Fenwick, and the rest of their company, [I say] I was to serve them only in the drawing, ordering and making of a city, towns or forts of defence. And so I came from Holland to London, and from thence to New-England, where I was appointed to attend such orders as Mr. John Winthrop, Esquire, the present Governor of Conectecott, was to appoint, whether at Pequit [Pequot] river, or Conectecott, and that we should choose a place both for the convenience of a good harbour, and also for capableness and fitness for fortification. But I landing at Boston the latter end of November, the aforesaid Mr. Winthrop had sent before one Lieut. Gibbons, Sergeant Willard, with some carpenters, to take possession of the River's mouth, where they began to build houses against the Spring; we expecting, according to promise, that there would have come from England to us 300 able men, whereof 200 should attend fortification, 50 to till the ground, and 50 to build houses. But our great expectation at the River's mouth, came only to two men, viz. Mr. Fenwick, and his man, who came with Mr. Hugh Peters, and Mr. Oldham and Thomas Stanton, bringing with them some Otterskin coats, and Beaver, and skeins of wampum, which the Pequits [Pequots] had sent for a present, because the English had required those Pequits [Pequots] that had killed a Virginean [Virginian], one Capt. Stone, with his Bark's crew, in Conectecott River, for they said they would have their lives and not their presents; then I answered, Seeing you will take Mr. Winthrop to the Bay to see his wife, newly brought to bed of her first child, and though you say he shall return, yet I know if you make war with these Pequits, he will not come hither again, for I know you will keep yourselves safe, as you think, in the Bay. but myself, with these few, you will leave at the stake to be roasted, or for hunger to be starved, for Indian corn is now 12,9. per bushel, and we have but three acres planted, and if they will now make war for a Virginian and expose us to the Indians, whose mercies are cruelties, they, I say, they love the Virginians better than us: for, have they stayed these four or five years, and will they begin now, we being so few in the River, and have scarce holes to put our heads in? I pray ask the Magistrates in the Bay if they have forgot what I said to them when I returned from Salem? For Mr. Winthrop, Mr. Haines, Mr. Dudley, Mr. Ludlow, Mr. Humfry, Mr. Belingam [Bellingham], Mr. Coddington, and Mr. Nowell; — these entreated me to go with Mr. Humfry and Mr. Peters to view the country, to see how fit it was for fortification. And I told them that Nature had done more than half the work already, and I thought no' foreign potent enemy would do them any hurt, but one that was near. They asked me who that was, and I said it was Capt. Hunger that threatened them most, for, (said I,) War is like a three-footed Stool, want one foot and down comes all; and these three feet are men, victuals, and munition, therefore, seeing in peace you are like to be famished, what will or can be done if war? Therefore I think, said I, it will be best only to fight against Capt. Hunger, and let fortification alone awhile; and if need hereafter require it, I can come to do you any service: and they all liked my saying well. Entreat them to rest awhile, till we get more strength here about us, and that we hear where the seat of the war will be, may approve of it, and provide for it, for I had but twenty-four in all, men, women, and boys and girls, and not food for them for two months, unless we saved our corn-field, which could not possibly be if they came to war, for it is two miles from our home. Mr. Winthrop, Mr. Fenwick, and Mr. Peters promised me that they would do their utmost endeavour to persuade the Bay-men to desist from war a year or two, till we could be better provided for it; and then the Pequit Sachem was sent for, and the present returned, but full sore against my will. So they three returned to Boston, and two or three days after came an Indian from Pequit, whose name was Cocommithus, who had lived at Plimoth, and could speak good English; he desired that Mr. Steven [Stephen] Winthrop would go to Pequit with an £100 worth of trucking cloth and all other trading ware, for they knew that we had a great cargo of goods of Mr. Pincheon's, and Mr. Steven Winthrop had the disposing of it. And he said that if he would come he might put off all his goods, and the Pequit Sachem would give him two horses that had been there a great while. So I sent the Shallop, with Mr. Steven Winthrop, Sergeant Tille [Tilly], (whom we called afterward Sergeant Kettle, because he put the kettle on his head,) and Thomas Hurlbut and three men more, charging them that they should ride in the middle of the river, and not go ashore until they had done all their trade, and that Mr. Steven Winthrop should stand in the hold of the boat, having their guns by them, and swords by their sides, the other four to be, two in the fore cuddie, and two in aft, being armed in like manner, that so they out of the loop-holes might clear the boat, if they were by the Pequits assaulted; and that they should let but one canoe come aboard at once, with no more but four Indians in her, and when she had traded then another, and that they should lie no longer there than one day, and at night to go out of the river; and if they brought the two horses, to take them in at a clear piece of land at the mouth of the River, two of them go ashore to help the horses in, and the rest stand ready with their guns in their hands, if need were, to defend them from the Pequits, for I durst not trust them. So they went and found but little trade, and they having forgotten what I charged them, Thomas Hurlbut and one more went ashore to boil the kettle, and Thomas Hurlbut stepping into the Sachem's wigwam, not far from the shore, enquiring for the horses, the Indians went out of the wigwam, and Wincumbone, his mother's sister, was then the great Pequit Sachem's wife, who made signs to him that he should be gone, for they would cut off his head; which, when he perceived, he drew his sword ran to the others, and got aboard, and immediately came abundance of Indians to the water-side and called them to come ashore, but they immediately set sail and came home, and this caused me to keep watch and ward, for I saw they plotted our destruction. And suddenly after came Capt. Endecott, Capt. Turner, and Capt. Undrill [Underhill], with a company of soldiers, well fitted, to Seabrook, and made that place their rendezvous or seat of war, and that to my great grief, for, said I, you come hither to raise these wasps about my ears, and then you will take wing and flee away; but when I had seen their commission I wondered, and made many allegations against the manner of it, but go they did to Pequit, and as they came without acquainting any of us in the River with it, so they went against our will, for I knew that I should lose our corn-field; then I entreated them to hear what I would say to them, which was this: Sirs, Seeing you will go, I pray you, if you don't load your Barks with Pequits, load them with corn, for that is now gathered with them, and dry, ready to put into their barns, and both you and we have need of it, and I will send my shallop and hire this Dutchman's boat, there present, to go with you, and if you cannot attain your end of the Pequits, yet you may load your barks with corn, which will be welcome to Boston and to me: But they said they had no bags to load them with, then said I, here is three dozen of new bags, you shall have thirty of them, and my shallop to carry them, and six of them my men shall use themselves, for I will with the Dutchmen send twelve men well provided; and I desired them to divide the men into three parts, viz. two parts to stand without the corn, and to defend the other one third part, that carried the corn to the water-side, till they have loaded what they can. And the men there in arms, when the rest are aboard, shall in order go aboard, the rest that are aboard shall with their arms clear the shore, if the Peqnits do assault them in the rear, and then, when the General shall display his colours, all to set sail together. To this motion they all agreed, and I put the three dozen of bags aboard my shallop, and away they went, and demanded the Pequit Sachem to come into parley. But it was returned for answer, that he was from home, but within three hours he would come; and so from three to six, and thence to nine, there came none. But the Indians came without arms to our men, in great numbers, and they talked with my men, whom they knew; but in the end, at a word given, they all on a sudden ran away from our men, as they stood in rank and file, and not an Indian more was to be seen: and all this while before, they carried all their stuff away, and thus was that great parley ended. Then they displayed their colours, and beat their drums, burnt some wigwams and some heaps of corn, and my men carried as much aboard as they could, but the army went aboard, leaving my men ashore, which ought to have marched aboard first. But they all set sail, and my men were pursued by the Indians, and they hurt some of the Indians, and two of them came home wounded. The Bay-men killed not a man, save that one Kichomiquim [Cutshamequinl, an Indian Sachem of the Bay, killed a Pequit; and thus began the war between the Indians and us in these parts. So my men being come home, and having brought a pretty quantity of corn with them, they informed me (both Dutch and English) of all passages. I was glad of the corn. After this I immediately took men and went to our corn-field, to gather our corn^ appointing others to come about with the shallop and fetch it, and left five lusty men in the strong-house, with long guns, which house I had built for the defence of the corn. Now these men not regarding the charge I had given them, three of them went a mile from the house a fowling; and having loaded themselves with fowl they returned. But the Pequits let them pass first, till they had loaded themselves, but at their return they arose out of their ambush, and shot them all three; one of them escaped through the corn, shot through the leg, the other two they tormented. Then the next day I sent the shallop to fetch the five men, and the rest of the corn that was broken down, and they found but three, as is above said, and when they had gotten that they left the rest; and as soon as they were gone a little way from shore, they saw the house on fire. Now so soon as the boat came home, and brought us this bad news, old Mr. Michell was very urgent with me to lend him the boat to fetch hay home from the Six-mile Island, but I told him they were too few men, for his four men could but carry the hay aboard, and one must stand in the boat to defend them, and they must have two more at the foot of the Rock, with their guns, to keep the Indians from running down upon them. And in the first place, before they carry any of the cocks of hay, to scour the meadow with their three dogs,— to march all abreast from the lower end up to the Rock, and if they found the meadow clear, then to load their hay; but this was also neglected, for they all went ashore and fell to carrying off their hay, and the Indians presently rose out of the long grass, and killed three, and took the brother of Mr. Michell, who is the minister of Cambridge, and roasted him alive; and so they served a shallop of his, coming down the river in the Spring, having two men, one whereof they killed at Six-mile Island, the other came down drowned to us ashore at our doors, with an arrow shot into his eye through his head.

In the 22d of February, I went out with ten men, and three dogs, half a mile from the house, to burn the weeds, leaves and reeds, upon the neck of land, because we had felled twenty timber-trees, which we were to roll to the water-side to bring home, every man carrying a length of match with brimstonematches with him to kindle the fire withal. But when we came to the small of the Neck, the weeds burning, I having before this set two sentinels on the small of the Neck, I called to the men that were burning the reeds to come away, but they would not until they had burnt up the rest of their matches. Presently there starts up four Indians out of the fiery reeds, but ran away, I calling to the rest of our men to come away out of the marsh. Then Robert Chapman and Thomas Hurlbut, being sentinels, called to me, saying there came a number of Indians out of the other side of the marsh. Then I went to stop them, that they should not get the wood-land; but Thomas Hurlbut cried out to me that some of the men did not follow me, for Thomas Rumble and Arthur Branch, threw down their two guns and ran away; then the Indians shot two of them that were in the reeds, and sought to get between us and home, but durst not come before us, but kept us in a half - moon, we retreating and exchanging many a shot, so that Thomas Hurlbut was shot almost through the thigh, John Spencer in the back, into his kidneys, myself into the thigh, two more were shot dead. But in our retreat I kept Hurlbut and Spencer still before us, we defending ourselves with our naked swords, or else they had taken us all alive, so that the two sore wounded men, by our slow retreat, got home with their guns, when our two sound men ran away and left their guns behind them. But when I saw the cowards that left us, I resolved to let them draw lots which of them should be hanged, for the articles did hang up in the hall for them to read, and they knew they had been published long before. But at the intercession of old Mr. Michell, Mr. Higgisson [Higginson], and Mr. Pell, I did forbear. Within a few days after, when I had cured myself of my wound, I went out with eight men to get some fowl for our relief, and found the guns that were thrown away, and the body of one man shot through, the arrow going in at the right side, the head sticking fast, half through a rib on the left side, which I took out and cleansed it, and presumed to send to the Bay, because they had said that the arrows of the Indians were of no force.

Anthony Dike, master of a bark, having his bark at Rhode Island in the winter, was sent by Mr. Vane, then Governor. Anthony came to Rhode-Island by land, and from thence he came with his bark to me with a letter, wherein was desired that I should consider and prescribe the best way I could to quell these Pequits, which I also did, and with my letter sent the man's rib as a token. A few days after, came Thomas Stanton down the River, and staying for a wind, while he was there came a troop of Indians within musket shot, laying themselves and their arms down behind a little rising hill and two great trees; which I perceiving, called the carpenter whom I had shewed how to charge and level a gun, and that he should put two cartridges of musket bullets into two sakers guns that lay about; and we levelled them against the place, and I told him that he must look towards me, and when he saw me wave my hat above my head he should give fire to both the guns; then presently came three Indians, creeping out and calling to us to speak with us: and I was glad that Thomas Stanton was there, and I sent six men down by the Garden Pales to look that none should come under the hill behind us; and having placed the rest in places convenient closely, Thomas and I with my sword, pistol and carbine, went ten or twelve pole without the gate to parley with them. And when the six men came to the Garden Pales, at the corner, they found a great number of Indians creeping behind the fort, or betwixt us and home, but they ran away. Now I had said to Thomas Stanton, Whatsoever they say to you, tell me first, for we will not answer them directly to any thing, for I know not the mind of the rest of the English. So they came forth, calling us nearer to them, and we them nearer to us. But I would not let Thomas go any further than the great stump of a tree, and I stood by him; then they asked who we were, and he answered, Thomas and Lieutenant. But they said he lied, for I was shot with many arrows; and so I was, but my buff coat preserved me, only one hurt me. But when I spake to them they knew my voice, for one of them had dwelt three months with us, but ran away when the Bay-men came first. Then they asked us if we would fight with Niantecut Indians, for they were our friends and came to trade with us. We said we knew not the Indians one from another, and therefore would trade with none. Then they said, Have you fought enough? We said we knew not yet. Then they asked if we did use to kill women and children? We said they should see that hereafter. So they were silent a small space, and then they said, We are Pequits, and have killed Englishmen, and can kill them as mosquetoes, and we will go to Conectecott and kill men, women, and children, and we will take away the horses, cows and hogs. When Thomas Stanton had told me this, he prayed me to shoot that rogue, for, said he, he hath an Englishman's coat on, and saith that he hath killed three, and these other four have their cloathes on their backs. I said, No, it is not the manner of a parley, but have patience and I shall fit them ere they go. Nay, now or never, said he; so when he could get no other answer but this last, I bid him tell them that they should not go to Conectecott, for if they did kill all the men, and take all the rest as they said, it would do them no good, but hurt, for English women are lazy, and can't do their work; horses and cows will spoil your corn-fields, and the hogs their clam -banks, and so undo them: then I pointed to our great house, and bid him tell them there lay twenty pieces of trucking cloth, of Mr. Pincheon's, with hoes, hatchets, and all manner of trade, they were better fight still with us, and so get all that, and then go up the river after they had killed all us. Having heard this, they were mad as dogs, and ran away; then when they came to the place from whence they came, I waved my hat about my head, and the two great guns went off, so that there was a great hubbub amongst them. Then two days after, came down Capt. Mason, and Sergeant Seely, with five men more, to see how it was with us; and whilst they were there, came down a Dutch boat, telling us the Indians had killed fourteen English, for by that boat I had sent up letters to Conectecott, what I heard, and what I thought, and how to prevent that threatened danger, and received back again rather a scoff, than any thanks, for my care and pains. But as I wrote, so it fell out to my great grief and theirs, for the next, or second day after, (as Major Mason well knows,) came down a great many canoes, going down the creek beyond the marsh, before the fort, many of them having white shirts; then I commanded the carpenter whom I had shewed to level great guns, to put in two round shot into the two sackers, and we levelled them at a certain place, and I stood to bid him give fire, when I thought the canoe would meet the bullet, and one of them took off the nose of a great canoe wherein the two maids were, that were taken by the Indians, whom I redeemed and clothed, for the Dutchmen, whom I sent to fetch them, brought them away almost naked from Pequit, they putting on their own linen jackets to cover their nakedness; and though the redemption cost me ten pounds, I am yet to have thanks for my care and charge about them: these things are known to Major Mason.

Then came from the Bay Mr. Tille, with a permit to go up to Harford [Hartford], and coming ashore he saw a paper nailed up over the gate, whereon was written, that no boat or bark should pass the fort, but that they come to an anchor first, that I might see whether they were armed and manned sufficiently, and they were not to land any where after they passed the fort till they came to Wethersfield; and this I did because Mr. Mitch el had lost a shallop before coming down from Wethersfield, with three men well armed. This Mr. Tille gave me ill language for my presumption, (as he called it), with other expressions too long here to write. When he had done, I bid him go to his warehouse, which he had built before I come, to fetch his goods from thence, for I would watch no longer over it. So he, knowing nothing, went and found his house burnt, and one of Mr. Plum's with others, and he told me to my face that I had caused it to be done; but Mr. Higgisson, Mr. Pell, Thomas Hurlbut and John Green can witness that the same day that our house was burnt at Cornfield-point I went with Mr. Higgisson, Mr. Pell, and four men more, broke open a door and took a note of all that was in the house and gave it to Mr. Higgisson to keep, and so brought all the goods to our house, and delivered it all to them again when they came for it, without any penny of charge. Now the very next day after I had taken the goods out, before the sun was quite down, and we all together in the great hall, all them houses were on fire in one instant. The Indians ran away, but I would not follow them. Now when Mr. Tille had received all his goods I said unto him, I thought I had deserved for my honest care both for their bodies and goods of those that passed by here, at the least better language, and am resolved to order such malepert persons as you are; therefore I wish you and also charge you to observe that which you have read at the gate, 'tis my duty to God, my masters, and my love I bear to you all which is the ground of this, had you but eyes to see it; but you will not till you feel it. So he went up the river, and when he came down again to his place, which I called Tille's folly, now called Tille's point, in our sight in despite, having a fair wind he came to an anchor, and with one man more went ashore, discharged his gun, and the Indians fell upon him, and killed the other, and carried him alive over the river in our sight, before my shallop could come to them; for immediately I sent seven men to fetch the Pink down, or else it had been taken and three men more. So they brought her down, and I sent Mr. Higgisson and Mr. Pell aboard to take an invoice of all that was in the vessel, that nothing might be lost. Two days after came to me, as I had written to Sir Henerie Vane, then Governor of the Bay, I say came to me Capt, Undrill [Underbill], with twenty lusty men, well armed, to stay with me two months, or 'till something should be done about the Pequits. He came at the charge of my masters. Soon after came down from Harford Maj. Mason, Lieut. Seely, accompanied with Mr. Stone and eighty Englishmen, and eighty Indians, with a commission. from Mr. Ludlow and Mr. Steel, and some others; these came to go fight with the Pequits. But when Capt. Undrill [Underhill] and I had seen their commission, we both said they were not fitted for such a design, and we said to Maj. Mason we wondered he would venture himself, being no better fitted; and he said the Magistrates could not or would not send better; then we said that none of our men should go with them, neither should they go unless we, that were bred soldiers from our youth, could see some likelihood to do better than the Baymen with their strong commission last year. Then I asked them how they durst trust the Mohegin [Mohegan] Indians, who had but that year come from the Pequits. They said they would trust them, for they could not well go without them for want of guides. Yea, said I, but I will try them before a man of ours shall go with you or them; and I called for Uncas and said unto him, You say you will help Maj. Mason, but I will first see it, therefore send you now twenty men to the Bass river, for there went yesternight six Indians in a canoe thither; fetch them now dead or alive, and then you shall go with Maj. Mason, else not. So he sent his men who killed four, brought one a traitor to us alive, whose name was Kiswas, and one ran away. And I gave him fifteen yards of trading cloth on my own charge, to give unto his men according to their desert. And having staid there five or six days before we could agree, at last we old soldiers agreed about the way and act, and took twenty insufficient men from the eighty that came from Harford [Hartford] and sent them up again in a shallop, and Capt. Undrill [Underhill] with twenty of the lustiest of our men went in their room, and I furnished them with such things as they wanted, and sent Mr. Pell, the sergeon, with them; and the Lord God blessed their design and way, so that they returned with victory to the glory of God, and honour of our nation, having slain three hundred, burnt their fort, and taken many prisoners. Then came to me an Indian called Wequash, and I by Mr. Higgisson inquired of him, how many of the Pequits were yet alive that had helped to kill Englishmen; and he declared them to Mr. Higgisson, and he writ them down, as may appear by his own hand here enclosed, and I did as therein is written. Then three days after the fight came Waiandance, next brother to the old Sachem of Long Island, and having been recommended to me by Maj. Gibbons, he came to know if we were angry with all Indians. I answered No, but only with such as had killed Englishmen. He asked me whether they that lived upon Long -Island might come to trade with us. I said No, nor we with them, for if I should send my boat to trade for corn, and you have Pequits with you, and if my boat should come into some creek by reason of bad weather, they might kill my men, and I shall think that you of Long Island have done it, and so we may kill all you for the Pequits; but if you will kill all the Pequits that come to you, and send me their heads, then I will give to you as to Weakwash [Wequash], and you shall have trade with us. Then, said he, I will go to my brother, for he is the great Sachem of all Long Island, and if we may have peace and trade with you, we will give you tribute, as we did the Pequits. Then I said, If you have any Indians that have killed English, yon must bring their heads also. He answered, not any one, and said that Gibbons, my brother, would have told you if it had been so; so he went away and did as I had said, and sent me five heads, three and four heads for which I paid them that brought them as I had promised.

Then came Capt. Stoten [Stoughton] with an army of 300 men, from the Bay, to kill the Pequits; but they were fled beyond New Haven to a swamp. I sent Wequash after them, who went by night to spy them out, and the army followed him, and found them at the great swamp, who killed some and took others, and the rest fled to the Mowhakues [Mohawks], with their Sachem. Then the Mohawks cut off his head and sent it to Hartford, for then they all feared us, but now it is otherwise, for they say to our faces that our Commissioners meeting once a year, and speak a great deal, or write a letter, and there' s all, for they dare not fight. But before they went to the Great Swamp they sent Thomas Stanton over to Long Island and Shelter Island to find Pequits there, but there was none, for the Sachem Waiandance, that was at Plimoth when the Commissioners were there, and set there last, I say, he had killed so many of the Pequits, and sent their heads to me, that they durst not come there; and he and his men went with the English to the Swamp, and thus the Pequits were quelled at that time. But there was like to be a great broil between Miantenomie [Miantunnomoh] and Unchus [Uncas] who should have the rest of the Pequits, but we meditated between them and pacified them; also Unchus challenged the Narraganset Sachem out to a single combat, but he would not fight without all his men; but they were pacified, though the old grudge remained still, as it doth appear. Thus far I had written in a book, that all men and posterity might know how and why so many honest men had their blood shed, yea, and some flayed alive, others cut in pieces, and some roasted alive, only because Kichamokin [Cutshamequin], a Bay Indian, killed one Pequit; and thus far of the Pequit war, which was but a comedy in comparison of the tragedies which hath been here threatened since, and may yet come, if God do not open the eyes, ears, and hearts of some that I think are wilfully deaf and blind, and think because there is no change that the vision fails, and put the evil -threatened day far off, for say they, We are now twenty to one to what we were then, and none dare meddle with us. Oh! wo be to the pride and security which hath been the ruin of many nations, as woful experience has proved.

But I wonder, and so doth many more with me, that the Bay doth no better revenge the murdering of Mr. Oldham, an honest man of their own, seeing they were at such cost for a Virginian. The Narragansets that were at Block-Island killed him, and had £50 of gold of his, for I saw it when he had five pieces of me, and put it up into a clout and tied it up all together, when he went away from me to Block Island; but the Narragansets had it and punched holes into it, and put it about their necks for jewels; and afterwards I saw the Dutch have some of it, which they had of the Narragansets at a small rate.

And now I find that to be true which our Waiandance told me many years ago, and that was this; that seeing all the plots of the Narragansets were always discovered, he said they would let us alone 'till they had destroyed Uncas, and him, and then they, with the Mowquakes and Mowhakues and the Indians beyond the Dutch, and all the Northern and Eastern Indians, would easily destroy us, man and mother's son. This have I informed the Governors of these parts, but all in vain, for I see they have done as those of Wethersfield, not regarding till they were impelled to it by blood; and thus we may be sure of the fattest of the flock are like to go first, if not altogether, and then it will be too late to read Jer. xxv. — for drink we shall if the Lord be not the more merciful to us for our extreme pride and base security, which cannot but stink before the Lord; and we may expect this, that if there should be war again between England and Holland, our friends at the Dutch and our Dutch Englishmen would prove as true to us now, as they were when the fleet came out of England; but no more of that, a word to the wise is enough.

And now I am old, I would fain die a natural death, or like a soldier in the field, with honor, and not to have a sharp stake set in the ground, and thrust into my fundament, and to have my skin flayed off by piecemeal, and cut in pieces and bits, and my flesh roasted and thrust down my throat, as these people have done, and I know will be done to the chief est in the country by hundreds, if God should deliver us into their hands, as justly he may for our sins.

I going over to Meantacut, upon the eastern end of Long Island, upon some occasion that I had there, I found four Narragansets there talking with the Sachem and his old counsellors. I asked an Indian what they were? He said that they were Narragansets, and that one was Miannemo [Miantunnomoh], a Sachem. What came they for? said I. He said he knew not, for they talked secretly; so I departed to another wigwam. Shortly after came the Sachem Waiandance to me and said, Do you know what these came for? No, said I; then he said, They say I must give no more wampum to the English, for they are no Sachems, nor none of their children shall be in their place if they die; and they have no tribute given them; there is but one king in England, who is over them all, and if you would send him 100,000 fathom of wampum, he would not give you a knife for it, nor thank you. And I said to them, Then they will come and kill us all, as they did the Pequits; then they said No, the Pequits gave them wampum and beaver, which they loved so well, but they sent it them again, and killed them because they had killed an Englishman; but you have killed none, therefore give them nothing. Now friend, tell me what I shall say to them, for one of them is a great man. Then said I, Tell them that you must go first to the farther end of LongIsland, and speak with all the rest, and a month hence you will give them an answer. Mean time you may go to Mr. Haines, and he will tell you what to do, and I will write all this now in my book that I have here; and so he did, and the Narragansets departed, and this Sachem came to me at my house, and I wrote this matter to Mr. Haines, and he went up with it to Mr. Haines, who forbid him to give any thing to the Narraganset, and writ to me so. — And when they came again they came by my Island, and I knew them to be the same men; and I told them they might go home again, and I gave them Mr. Haynes his letter for Mr. Williams to read to the Sachem. So they returned back again, for I had said to them, that if they would go to Mantacut I would go likewise with them, and that Long-Island must not give wampum to Narraganset.

A while after this came Miantenomie from BlockIsland to Mantacut with a troop of men, Waiandance being not at home; and instead of receiving presents, which they used to do in their progress, he gave them gifts, calling them brethren and friends, for so are we all Indians as the English are, and say brother to one another; so must we be one as they are, otherwise we shall be all gone shortly, for you know our fathers had plenty of deer and skins, our plains were full of deer, as also our woods, and of turkies, and our coves full of fish and fowl. But these English having gotten our land, they with scythes cut down the grass, and with axes fell the trees; their cows and horses eat the grass, and their hogs spoil our clam banks, and we shall all be starved; therefore it is best for you to do as we, for we are all the Sachems from east to west, both Moquakues and Mohauks joining with us, and we are all resolved to fall upon them all, at one appointed day; and therefore I am come to you privately first, because you can persuade the Indians and Sachem to what you will, and I will send over fifty Indians to Block-Island, and thirty to you from thence, and take an hundred of Southampton Indians with gardener's narrative. 143 an hundred of your own here; and when you see the three fires that will be made forty days hence, in a clear night, then do as we, and the next day fall on and kill men, women, and children, but no cows, for they will serve to eat till our deer be increased again. — And our old men thought it was well. So the Sachem came home and had but little talk with them, yet he was told there had been a secret consultation between the old men and Miantenomie, but they told him nothing in three days. So he came over to me and acquainted me with the manner of the Narragansets being there with his men, and asked me what I thought of it; and I told him that the Narraganset Sachem was naught to talk with his men secretly in his absence, and I bid him go home, and told him a way how he might know all, and then he should come and tell me; and so he did, and found out all as is above written, and I sent intelligence of it over to Mr. Haynes and Mr. Eaton; but because my boat was gone from home it was fifteen days before they had any letter, and Miantenomie was gotten home before they had news of it. And the old men, when they saw how I and the Sachem had beguiled them, and that he was come over to me, they sent secretly a canoe over, in a moon-shine night, to Narraganset to tell them all was discovered; so the plot failed, blessed be God, and the plotter, next Spring after, did as Ahab did at Ramoth-Gilead.— So he to Mohegin, and there had his fall.

Two years after this, Ninechrat sent over a captain of his, who acted in every point as the former; him the Sachem took and bound and brought him to me, and I wrote the same to Governor Eaton, and sent an Indian that was my servant and had lived four years with me; him, with nine more, I sent to carry him to New-Haven, and gave them food for ten days. But the wind hindered them at Plum-Island; then they went to Shelter-Island, where the old Sachem dwelt — Waiandance's elder brother, and in the night they let him go, only my letter they sent to New-Haven, and thus these two plots was discovered; but now my friend and brother is gone, who will now do the like?

But if the premises be not sufficient to prove Waiandance a true friend to the English, for some may say he did all this out of malice to the Pequits and Narragansets; now I shall prove the like with respect to the Long-Islanders, his own men. For I being at Meantacut, it happened that for an old grudge of a Pequit, who was put to death at Southampton, being known to be a murderer, and for this his friends bear a spite against the English. So as it came to pass at that day I was at Mantacut, a good honest woman was killed by them at Southampton, but it was not known then who did this murder. And the brother of this Sachem was Shinacock Sachem could or would not find it out. At that time Mr. Gosmore and Mr. Howell, being magistrates, sent an Indian to fetch the Sachem thither; and it being in the night, I was laid down when he came, and being a great cry amongst them, upon which all the men gathered together, and the story being told, all of them said the Sachem should not go, for, said they, they will either bind you or kill you, and then us, both men, women and children; therefore let your brother find it out, or let them kill you and us, we will live and die together. So there was a great silence for a while, and then the Sachem said, Now you have all done I will hear what my friend will say, for [he] knows what they will do. So they wakened me as they thought, but I was not asleep, and told me the story, but I made strange of the matter, and said, If the magistrates have sent for you why do you not go? They will bind me or kill me, saith he. I think so, said I, if you have killed the woman, or known of it, and did not reveal it; but you were here and did it not. But was any of your Mantauket Indians there to-day? They all answered, Not a man these two days, for we have inquired concerning that already. Then said I, Did none of you ever hear any Indian say he would kill English? — No, said they all; then I said, I shall not go home 'till tomorrow, though I thought to have been gone so soon as the moon was up, but I will stay here till you all know it is well with your Sachem; if they bind him, bind me, and if they kill him, kill me. But then you must find out him that did the murder, and all that know of it, them they will have and no more. Then they with a great cry thanked me, and I wrote a small note with the Sachem, that they should not stay him long in their houses, but let him eat and drink and be gone, for he had his way before him. So they did, and that night he found out four that were consenters to it, and knew of it, and brought them to them at Southampton, and they were all hanged at Harford, whereof one of these was a great man among them, commonly called the Blue Sachem.

A further instance of his faithfulness is this; about the Pequit war time one William Hamman [Hammond], of the Bay, killed by a giant-like Indian towards the Dutch. I heard of it, and told Waiandance that he must kill him or bring him to me; but he said it was not his brother's mind, and he is the great Sachem of all Long-Island, likewise the Indian is a mighty great man, and no man durst meddle with him, and hath many friends. So this rested until he had killed another, one Thomas Famngton. After this the old Sachem died, and I spake to this Sachem again about it, and he answered, He is so cunning, that when he hears that I come that way a hunting, that his friends tell him, and then he is gone. — But I will go at some time when nobody knows of it, and then I will kill him; and so he did — and this was the last act which he did for us, for in the time of a great mortality among them he died, but it was by poison; also two thirds of the Indians upon Long-Island died, else the Narragansets had not made such havoc here as they have, and might not help them. — And this I have written chiefly for our own good, that we might consider what danger we are all in, and also to declare to the country that we have found an heathen, yea an Indian, in this respect to parallel the Jewish Mordecai. But now I am at a stand, for all we English would be thought and called Christians; yet, though I have seen this before spoken, having been these twenty-four years in the mouth of the premises, yet I know not where to find, or whose name to insert, to parallel Ahasuerus lying on his bed and could not sleep, and called for the Chronicles to be read; and when he heard Mordecai named, said, What hath been done for him? But who will say as he said, or do answerable to what he did? But our New-England twelvepenny Chronicle is stuffed with a catalogue of the names of some, as if they had deserved immortal fame; but the right New-England military worthies are left out for want of room, as Maj. Mason, Capt. Undrill [Underhill], Lieut. Sielly

92

[Seely], &c, who undertook the desperate way and design to Mistick Fort, and killed three hundred, burnt the fort and took many prisoners, though they are not once named. But honest Abraham thought it no shame to name the confederates that helped him to war when he redeemed his brother Lot; but Uncas of Mistick, and Waiandance, at the Great Swamp and ever since your trusty friend, is forgotten, and for our sakes persecuted to this day with fire and sword, and Ahasuerus of New-England is still asleep, and if there be any like to Ahasuerus, let him remember what glory to God and honor to our nation hath followed their wisdom and valor. Awake! awake Ahasuerus, if there be any of thy seed or spirit here, and let not Haman destroy us as he hath done our Mordecai! And although there hath been much blood shed here in these parts among us, God and we know it came not by us. But if all must drink of this cup that is threatened, then shortly the king of Sheshack shall drink last, and tremble and fall when our pain will be past. O that I were in the countries again, that in their but twelve years truce, repaired cities and towns, made strong forts, and prepared all things needful against a time of war like Solomon. I think the soil hath almost infected me, but what they or our enemies will do hereafter I know not. I hope I shall not live so long to hear or see it, for I am old and out of date, else I might be in fear to see and hear that I think ere long will come upon us.

Thus for our tragical story, now to the comedy. When we were all at supper in the great hall, they (the Pequits) gave us alarm to draw us out three times before we could finish our short supper, for we had but little to eat, but you know that I would not go out; the reasons you know.

2ndly. You Robert Chapman, you know that when you and John Bagley were beating samp at the Garden Pales, the sentinels called you to run in, for there was a number of Pequits creeping to you to catch you; I hearing it went up to the Redoubt and put two cross-bar shot into the two guns that lay above, and levelled them at the trees in the middle of the limbs and boughs, and gave order to John Frend and his man to stand with hand-spikes to turn them this or that way, as they should hear the Indians shout, for they should know my shout from theirs for it should be very short. Then I called six men, and the dogs, and went out, running to the place, and keeping all abreast, in sight, close together. And when I saw my time I said, Stand! and called all to me saying, Look on me; and when I hold up my hand, then shout as loud as you can, and when I hold down my hand, then leave; and so they did. Then the Indians began a long shout, and then went off the two great guns and tore the limbs of the trees about their ears, so that divers of them were hurt, as may yet appear, for you told me when I was up at Harford this present year, 1 60, in the month of September, that there is one of them lyeth above Hartford, that is fain to creep on all four, and we shouted once or twice more; but they would not answer us again, so we returned home laughing. Another pretty prank we had with three great doors of ten feet long and four feet broad, being bored full of holes and driven full of long nails, as sharp as awl blades, sharpened by Thomas Hurlbut. — Then we placed in certain places where they should come, fearing lest they should come in the night and fire our redoubt or battery, and all the place, for we had seen then footing., where they had been in the night, when they shot at our sentinels, but could not hit them for the boards; and in a dry time and a dark night they came as they did before, and found the way a little too sharp for them; and as they skipped from one they trod upon another, and left the nails and doors dyed with their blood, which you know we saw the next morning, laughing at it.— And this I write that young men may learn, if they should meet with such trials as we met with there, and have not opportunity to cut off their enemies; yet they may, with such pretty pranks, preserve themselves from danger, — for policy is needful in wars as well as strength.

[1] Gardener arrived in Boston 28., Nov. 1635.
[2] He remained at Saybrook four years. A son was born to him 29., April 1636, which was the first white child born in Connecticut.